a visitor's guide to
new zealand
national parks

Kathy Ombler

NEW
HOLLAND

ıblishers (NZ) Ltd
ı

' Zealand
ِ6, Australia
ıited Kingdom
h Africa

Copyright © 2005 in text: Kathy Ombler
Copyright © 2005 in photography: Shaun Barnett, Darryn Pegram
    and Dave Hansford, as credited
Copyright © 2005 in maps: New Holland Publishers (UK) Ltd
Copyright © 2005 New Holland Publishers (NZ) Ltd

ISBN 1-86966-113-3

Managing editor: Matt Turner
Editing and design: Alison Dench
Cover design: Trevor Newman
Cartographic concept: John Loubser; DTP maps: John Hall
Additional cartography: Nick Keenleyside/Outline Draughting
Front cover photographs: Darryn Pegram/Black Robin Photography
Back cover photograph: Dave Hansford/Origin Natural History Media

10 9 8 7 6 5 4 3 2 1

Colour reproduction by Pica Digital Pte Ltd, Singapore
Printed by Times Offset (M) Sdn Bhd, Malaysia

A catalogue record for this book is available from the National
Library of New Zealand

Contents

Foreword

Kia ora

Human identity is strengthened by an affiliation with the environment. When you open the pages of this book you hold intrinsic taonga (treasures) of Aotearoa New Zealand in your hands and when you walk the pathways you are walking with our ancestors.

Our strikingly beautiful landscapes are more than the tangible that you can see and touch. There is the mystique and spirituality of the intangible that connects our people to the land and to our ancestors.

In 1887 my ancestor, Horonuku te Heuheu Tukino IV, gifted the sacred peaks of our mountains, Ruapehu, Tongariro and Ngauruhoe, to the nation and by this action – made solely for the preservation and retention of the natural and cultural values associated with this unique landscape – he created New Zealand's first national park. Tongariro is now listed as a World Heritage Area in recognition of those special natural and cultural values.

Our national park system has grown significantly since and the way in which we care for our landscapes is a matter of great importance. Experiencing and understanding natural places is a key to their protection and preservation.

Ka ū ki matanuku,
Ka ū ki matarangi,
Ka ū ki tēnei whenua
Hei whenua,
Māu e kai te manawa o tauhou!

I arrive where unknown earth is under my feet,
I arrive where a new sky is above me;
I arrive at this land, a resting place for me;
O spirit of earth! This stranger humbly
Offers his heart as food for you.

Tumu te Heuheu
Paramount Chief Ngāti Tūwharetoa
Head of New Zealand's Delegation to the World Heritage Committee

Acknowledgements

Special thanks to Department of Conservation staff throughout New Zealand for support, advice and checking screeds of draft text. Thanks also to Hineihaea Murphy and Pania Tahau (Haemata Ltd), Wendy Shaw (New Zealand Geographic Board), photographers Dave Hansford (Origin Natural History Media) and Shaun Barnett (Black Robin Photography), The Guild (special friends and colleagues), editor/ designer Alison Dench, managing editor Matt Turner, publisher Belinda Cooke and Stewart, Jenny, Sally and John Ombler for proof reading, listening and general encouragement.

Kathy Ombler

Introduction

New Zealand was the last major land mass to be settled by people, and one of the first countries in the world to establish a national park system. Thus significant areas of the country's magnificent natural landscapes, the mountains, glaciers, volcanoes, forests, lakes and rivers, and the diverse habitats therein, have long been protected.

While the conservation ethic has been strong from early times, so too has the desire to explore our national parks. Early traditions of climbing and tramping (hiking) continue today. The huge network of tracks, back-country huts and campsites that exists throughout New Zealand's 14 national parks is unparalleled. (Note that in New Zealand hiking or trekking is referred to as tramping, while the term 'track' is used to describe a trail.)

New Zealanders love exploring their own parks and sharing their finest features with visitors. A long tradition of guiding on historic tracks, such as the Milford in Fiordland, and on climbing routes in the mountains of Aoraki/Mt Cook, have expanded now into a multitude of tourism opportunities that cover all aspects of a visit to a national park: walking, climbing, cruising, kayaking, glacier walking, caving, nature tours, birdwatching, hunting and fishing.

National parks are managed by the Department of Conservation, subject to the National Parks Act 1980, policies of the New Zealand Conservation Authority and management plans prepared for each park.

The National Parks Act states that national parks are established to preserve in perpetuity natural areas of New Zealand for their intrinsic worth and so that the public may derive inspiration, enjoyment and recreation from the forests, mountains, fiords, lakes and rivers.

The Department of Conservation also manages other conservation land, including forest parks, scenic reserves, marine reserves and historic sites. Together with national parks, one-third of all New Zealand is protected as conservation land. The Department's Māori name is Te Papa Atawhai, which means 'to care for a treasure chest'. It is a name that reflects both the Department's responsibilities, and the affinity felt for conservation by the Māori people.

Providing for visitors and recreation in national parks is a major part of the Department's work. Facilities cater for all ages and fitness levels. Some of the most outstanding features of our national parks can be enjoyed on high-quality short walks that are suitable for wheelchairs. At the other extreme vast and specially designated wilderness areas, where no air access or built facilities are permitted, offer the chance for those who are able to explore remote valleys and mountains on nature's own terms.

New Zealand's national parks can be appreciated year-round, with obvious seasonal variations in scenery, wildlife watching and recreational experiences. In some parks tramping is better suited to summertime (November to March) when tracks and mountain passes are not covered by snow. In other lower-altitude, forest-covered parks, tracks are open year-round. Skiing is a winter recreation, climbing can be both, and avalanche danger in southern mountain parks is most prevalent in late winter and spring. Short walks, scenic cruises and wildlife watching are year-round activities.

National parks are open all year-round and can be visited free of charge and without a permit. However, payment is required for services, such as overnight stays in park huts and campsites, and permits or licences are required for activities such as hunting or fishing.

Licensed tourism operators offer a huge range of guided activities throughout the parks: walking, tramping, climbing, kayaking, nature appreciation, cave tours, scenic cruises, flights and drives, fishing, hunting, accommodation and transport services – and more.

General information

This book is a guide only, intended to be used alongside brochures, maps, advice from park staff and commercial tour operators.

Track classifications

Tracks range from sealed paths suitable for wheelchairs and strollers, to rough forest tracks or mountain routes marked only by occasional poles. There are five track categories that are used throughout New Zealand. These are clearly identified, often with the accompanying symbol, in park brochures and on park signs.

- Short Walk: well-formed, easy walking.

- Walking Track: well-formed, easy, longer walks.

- Great Walk and Easy Tramping Track: formed track for comfortable overnight tramping trips.

- Tramping Track: mostly unformed but have track directional markers, poles or cairns.

- Route: unformed, suitable only for experienced back-country walkers. Often above bushline and difficult to follow in poor visibility.

Great Walks

These are regarded as New Zealand's premier tramping tracks, showcasing some of the most outstanding scenery of all national parks. Huts and tracks on Great Walks are generally of a higher standard than other tracks, and many have booking systems to manage visitor pressures, thus every walker can enjoy his or her visit without worrying about overcrowding on the track or in the huts.

There are eight Great Walks (and one River Journey): Lake Waikaremoana Track, Tongariro Northern Circuit, Abel Tasman Coast Track, Heaphy Track, Routeburn Track, Milford Track, Kepler Track, Rakiura Track, and the Whanganui River Journey.

For most Great Walks there is a season, which lasts during the summer months from around October to April. At other times of the year facilities such as cooking equipment and fuel are taken out of some huts, and there is no resident warden. Some Great Walks (Tongariro Northern Circuit, Routeburn, Milford and Kepler) are generally snow-covered and suitable only for experienced climbers during winter.

Bookings for Great Walks can be made online through the Department of Conservation website www.doc.govt.nz, or in person at Department of Conservation visitor centres and some other agencies. Bookings can be made from 1 July, for the season immediately following.

Park huts

New Zealand's national parks have a huge network of back-country huts, of varying standard and design, and sharing these huts is a long tradition among trampers, climbers and hunters. Generally bunk space is available on a first-come, first-served basis, with people happily crowding together where necessary. Increased popularity has seen the introduction of booking systems for the most popular Great Walks tracks. In other huts, the first-come, first-served tradition stands.

Park huts are relatively basic; some offer cooking facilities by means of gas cookers. Except on some guided walks, there are no ready-cooked meals as found in the mountain inns of the European Alps. People therefore need to be self-sufficient, carrying their own bedding, food, cooking utensils and, in most cases, cooking stoves. This need not preclude another long-standing tradition: that of having 'a brew' – at the least some boiling water – ready to offer any new group arriving at the hut: a particularly welcome gesture in inclement conditions.

There are varying charges for park huts, depending on their categories and the facilities they offer. These vary from year to year, and the Department of Conservation's visitor centres and website provide the latest information.

Hut categories

There are four categories of park huts:

- Great Walks huts offer mattresses, water supply, sinks, toilets and heating with fuel. Some have solar lighting, cooking facilities with fuel (but no cooking utensils) and a resident warden during the Great Walks season.
- Serviced huts have bunks or sleeping platforms with mattresses, water supply, heating (and fuel during the peak season), toilet and sinks. Some have cooking facilities and a resident warden during the summer season.
- Standard huts have bunks or sleeping platforms with mattresses, a toilet and water supply. Wood-burning fires are provided at most huts below the bushline (with fuel, as in dead wood, collected by hut users).
- Basic huts and bivouacs (bivvies) provide very basic shelter with limited facilities. These are free to use.

Hut tickets, back-country hut passes (valid for one year for most huts and campsites but not Great Walks huts) and Great Walks passes can be purchased from any Department of Conservation visitor centre.

Campsites

There are four types of park camping areas with vehicle access, with fees varying according to the facilities they offer.

- Serviced campsites have flush toilets, tap water, showers, rubbish collection, picnic tables, mown grass and some powered sites. Many have barbecues or fireplaces, a kitchen, laundry and shop.

- Standard campsites (access to some is by boat only) have toilets, water supply, mown grass and possibly barbecues, picnic tables and rubbish collection.
- Informal campsites have a toilet, access to water and limited facilities. These are free of charge.
- There are also several camping areas provided along tramping tracks (some of the Great Walks campsites require bookings and a fee).

Being safe

Exploring New Zealand's national parks can be many things: enjoyable, uplifting, relaxing, challenging, inspiring – and seriously dangerous if things go wrong. It is important to be suitably prepared and equipped for whatever trip is planned. Match your proposed trip to your level of skill, fitness and equipment. If in doubt, join a commercially guided tour.

Weather

Be aware that New Zealand's back-country weather can change suddenly, at any time of the year. Travelling over open tussock tops, for example, can change dramatically from being an easy, sunny 'walk in the park' to a struggle for survival, with gales, freezing rain, white-outs and snow. Similarly, gentle, ankle-deep river crossings can become dangerous, raging torrents within hours.

Before your trip check the weather forecast, and ask about local conditions at the nearest park visitor centre. Be prepared to change plans, and be patient if the weather is bad and rivers are flooded. Be equipped for all weather conditions. At all times of the year take warm and waterproof clothing, first-aid kits and some emergency supplies.

Trip intentions

For day walks and overnight trips, let someone know where you are planning to go, and tell them when you have returned. Remember to leave details such as planned route, return date, party member names and vehicle details (if left at a road-end) with a responsible friend or park visitor centre. Trip intentions forms are available at park visitor centres or online at www.mountainsafety.org.nz. Fill in hut books during your trip, even if you do not stay in the hut. These details can assist search and rescue operations and may help save your life. Remember to check in again at the end of your trip.

Equipment

For serious tramping trips carry the relevant topographical maps (and know how to read them or have someone in your party who does), first-aid kit, survival kit and water bottle. Mountain radios, emergency position indicator beacons and satellite phones are available for hire. Mobile phone reception cannot be relied on in most areas of most national parks.

Lost?

Don't panic. Try to retrace your steps to the last place where you recognised the route. If your group is lost, stay together. Mark your position and only move within sight of this so you don't stray even further. Do not move around in white-out conditions or at night. Find the most sheltered spot you can, be it a large rock, lee side of a ridge or large tree, and stay put. Make your position as conspicuous as possible; for example, spread out bright-coloured clothing or survival bag.

Weather and safety websites

New Zealand weather service: www.metservice.co.nz
Avalanche warnings: www.avalanche.net.nz
Mountain Safety Council: www.mountainsafety.org.nz
Mountain radio suppliers: www.nzlsar.org.nz

Water

Clear running mountain water is generally safe for drinking, though the presence of giardia is a possibility. If unsure treat, filter or boil all water intended for drinking.

Environment

The Department of Conservation's Environmental Care Code asks visitors to:

- Protect plants and animals: Treat New Zealand's forests and birds with care and respect. They are unique and often rare.
- Remove rubbish: Litter is unattractive, harmful to wildlife and can increase vermin and disease. Plan your visits to reduce rubbish, and carry out what you carry in.
- Bury toilet waste: In areas without toilet facilities, bury your toilet waste in a shallow hole well away from waterways, tracks, campsites, and huts.
- Keep streams and lakes clean: When cleaning and washing, take the water and wash well away from the water source. Because soaps and detergents are harmful to water-life, drain used water into the soil to allow it to be filtered. If you suspect the water may be contaminated, boil it for at least three minutes, or filter it, or chemically treat it.
- Take care with fires: Portable fuel stoves are less harmful to the environment and are more efficient than fires. If you do use a fire, keep it small, use only dead wood and make sure it is out by dousing it with water and checking the ashes before leaving.
- Camp carefully: When camping, leave no trace of your visit.
- Keep to the track: By keeping to the track, where one exists, you lessen the chance of damaging fragile plants.
- Consider others: People visit the back country and rural areas for many reasons. Be considerate of other visitors who also have a right to enjoy the natural environment.
- Respect our cultural heritage: Many places in New Zealand have a spiritual and historical significance. Treat these places with consideration and respect.
- Enjoy your visit: Enjoy your outdoor experience. Take a last look before leaving an area: will the next visitor know that you have been there? Protect the environment for your own sake, for the sake of those who come after you, and for the environment itself.

Dangerous animals

New Zealand is one of the few countries in the world where there are no dangerous animals, poisonous snakes or similar such threats lurking in the outdoors. Wasps and a few species of poisonous spiders are the main wildlife threats in national parks, though pesky mosquitoes and sandflies have earned a fearsome reputation for the unwelcome attention they lavish on park visitors!

Vehicle safety

New Zealand's national parks are beautiful but, like anywhere in the world, some of its visitors are not. Sadly, theft from vehicles left at park tracks sometimes occurs. It is best not to leave vehicles parked overnight at park entrances, particularly at more isolated road-ends. Tramper shuttle transport is available for the most popular tramping tracks. Ask for car park advice from park visitor centres.

Dogs

To protect native wildlife, in particular ground-dwelling birds, it is an offence under the National Parks Act to bring dogs, or any introduced animals for that matter, into any national park.

Fires

In some parks fire can be a major threat. Trampers are encouraged to carry portable stoves. At the very least, please light fires only in fireplaces provided, and always extinguish fires after use.

Fishing

Rainbow and brown trout have been introduced into rivers and lakes throughout New Zealand, providing popular fishing opportunities in some national parks. Licences are required for fishing; these are available online at www.fishandgame.org.nz or phone 0800 LICENCE (0800 542 362) within New Zealand, 64-4-473 4838 from overseas, or purchase from selected sports shops and other agencies. Annual, winter season, 24-hour, family and junior licences are available. Fish and Game licences cover all of New Zealand except for the Taupō district, which is managed by the Department of Conservation. All native fish within national parks are protected.

Sea fishing presents something of an anomaly in this national park guide. The very essence of a national park is protection of all native species, yet in many areas adjacent to parks recreational sea fishing has long been popular, and around parks such as Rakiura National Park has provided a traditional livelihood for local residents.

The Royal Forest and Bird Society, New Zealand's largest environmental organisation, has issued a 'Best Fish Guide' that ranks the sustainability of seafood from the country's commercial fisheries. This guides consumers towards making purchases of fish from 'ecologically sustainable fisheries', taking into account the state of fish stocks, by-catch, damage to habitats and other ecological effects caused by the fishing. Interestingly, the guide also lists several fish recipes by leading New Zealand chefs. For information on obtaining the guide, check the website: www.forestandbird.org.nz.

When it comes to recreational sea fishing, it is important that people act responsibly. Be aware of legal limits as regards size and numbers of a particular species that can be caught. At the most, please catch enough for just one meal. For legal limits check the Ministry of Fisheries website: www.fish.govt.nz.

Hunting

Red deer were first introduced to New Zealand by early British settlers, keen to continue their hunting traditions of home. However, these animals thrived in the New Zealand bush, their numbers increased exponentially and their browsing of native vegetation caused serious damage to forests. Subsequent introductions of other deer species, plus wapiti, chamois, thar, pigs and goats, added to the impact. Professional government cullers reduced numbers during the 1960s. During the 1970s and 1980s a short-lived helicopter deer industry, culling animals for meat export then live capturing them for the development of a local deer farming industry, continued to hold numbers at bay.

Recreational hunting is encouraged in national parks and other conservation areas as a means of keeping animal numbers at a level that will not threaten the health of native forests and wildlife habitats. Hunting permits are required; these are available from park visitor centres and Department of Conservation offices. Only centre-fire rifles are permitted, no shotguns or .22 rifles. Hunting is restricted in some areas and during some seasons; for example, near popular tramping tracks. Hunting guides are available in many national parks.

Mountain biking

Mountain bikes are not permitted in national parks, except on formed roads. It is possible that new legislation might allow restricted mountain bike use in specified areas at some future, as yet undetermined, date. Mountain biking is permitted in some other conservation areas. Where there are good biking opportunities on park roads or in other areas close to specific parks, these are detailed in the relevant park chapter.

Tourism operators

All commercial ventures within a national park must be licensed with a Department of Conservation concession. This ensures the venture is compatible with the primary aim of protecting the special conservation values of national parks. It also ensures high standards are set, and that activities do not conflict with other visitors' enjoyment. All concessionaires are monitored to ensure they provide an environmentally sound, safe and educational experience. Every national park concessionaire also pays a percentage of the revenue they earn towards conservation work and maintenance of visitor facilities, thus every visitor who takes a guided walk or tour in a national park makes some contribution towards conservation.

Qualmark™

Qualmark™ is New Zealand's official quality standard for tourism operations, including those operating within national parks. All tourism operators who carry a Qualmark™ rating have been independently assessed. See www.qualmark.co.nz.

Green Globe 21

Many park concessionaires are also participants in Green Globe 21, an internationally recognised environmental certification programme for the tourism and travel industry. See www.greenglobe21.com.

Visitor information centres

There are Department of Conservation visitor information centres in or near all national parks, nearby towns and all major cities (see park chapters for contact details). Many of these have extensive displays and audiovisuals that educate and inform about the natural and historic features of the park. As well, most major towns – and many of the smaller tourist towns – have a visitor information centre which is part of New Zealand's official i-SITE network. See www.i-SITE.org.nz.

Other useful contacts

Department of Conservation www.doc.govt.nz

DOC Hotline (for reporting any safety hazards or conservation emergencies) freephone 0800 362 468

Tourism New Zealand www.newzealand.com

New Zealand Alpine Club www.alpineclub.org.nz

New Zealand Historic Places Trust www.historic.org.nz

Ornithological Society of New Zealand www.osnz.org.nz

New Zealand Mountain Guides Association www.nzmga.co.nz

Sea Kayak Operators Association of New Zealand www.seakayak.org.nz

Names of places, flora and fauna

Many places mentioned in this guide have both Māori and English names, such as Aoraki/Mt Cook and Stewart Island/Rakiura. These are legally recognised names that acknowledge both the original Māori name and association with these places, which are in many cases of special significance, and the English names later bestowed on them.

Most wildlife and plant species have both Māori and English names, and some have different Māori names in different tribal areas. In some cases the Māori name is more commonly used, in others the English. While the Māori names are gradually becoming more easily recognised, for the sake of clarity and simplicity this guide employs only the most commonly used names, be they Māori or English. The following list sets out some of the more widely known species and subspecies and their Māori and English names, generally with the better-known names listed first.

brown kiwi (in the North Island)
little spotted kiwi (mostly on
  Kapiti Island and some other
  sanctuaries)
great spotted kiwi, roroa
  (northern areas of the South
  Island)
Ōkārito brown kiwi, rowi
  (Ōkārito)
Haast tokoeka (South Westland,
  Mt Aspiring National Park)
southern tokoeka (Fiordland and
  Stewart Island/Rakiura)

North and South Island kākā,
  bush parrot
kea, mountain parrot
kākāpō, flightless ground parrot

yellow-crowned, red-crowned
  and orange-fronted parakeet,
  kākāriki
little blue penguin, kororā
yellow-eyed penguin, hoiho
Fiordland crested penguin,
  tawaki
white-flippered penguin,
  kororā (Banks Peninsula, near
  Christchurch)

tītī, muttonbird, sooty
  shearwater (Māori retain
  traditional harvesting rights
  for young tītī from islands
  around Stewart Island/
  Rakiura.)
white heron, kōtuku

royal spoonbill, kōtuku-
ngutupapa
blue duck, whio, kōwhiowhio
brown teal, pateke (plus three
subspecies on Great Barrier
Island, Auckland Islands and
Subantarctic Islands)
paradise shelduck, pūtangitangi
grey duck (heavily interbred with
introduced mallards)

North Island and Stewart Island
robin, toutouwai
South Island robin, kakaruai or
toutouwai
tomtit, South and North Island
tit and pied tit, miromiro
New Zealand pigeon, kererū or
kūkupa
rifleman, tītipounamu
bellbird, korimako
fantail, pīwakawaka
kōkako, blue-wattled crow
fernbird, mātā
takahē, flightless rail
grey warbler, riroriro
saddleback, tīeke

short-tailed and long-tailed bat,
pekapeka (New Zealand's only
native land mammals)

Hector's dolphin, tutumairekurai
(one of the world's two
smallest dolphin species)

Maui dolphin (the rarest and one
of the two smallest dolphins)
Dusky dolphin (in colder waters)
bottlenosed and common
dolphin (the most common of
nine dolphin species found in
New Zealand waters)
New Zealand fur seal, kekeno

crayfish, kōura, rock lobster (two
saltwater species, red rock and
packhorse, and nine smaller
freshwater species)
galaxiids, kōkopu, native trout
eel, tuna
sea egg, kina

beech, *Nothofagus*, tawai (There
are four species of beech: red,
hard, black and silver beech
and a subspecies, mountain
beech. Beech forest covers over
half the area of New Zealand's
native forests.)
podocarp, conifer (*Dacrydium*,
Podocarpus and *Dacrycaropus*,
including rimu, kahikatea,
miro, mataī and tōtara).

Further reading

A Tramper's Guide to New Zealand National Parks by Robbie Burton and Maggie Atkinson (reprinted Penguin, 1998)

Moir's Guide North, edited by Geoff Spearpoint (reprinted New Zealand Alpine Club, 2000)

Moir's Guide South, edited by Robin McNeill (reprinted Great Southern Lakes Press, 1995)

The Natural World of New Zealand by Gerard Hutching (Penguin, 2004)

Reed Field Guide to New Zealand Native Trees by John Salmond (Reed, 1999)

The Hand Guide to the Birds of New Zealand by Hugh Robertson and Barry Heather (Oxford University Press, 2001)

The Lord of the Rings Location Guidebook Extended Edition by Ian Brodie (HarperCollins, 2004)

New Zealand Encounter Outdoor Directory (Jasons 2005) available also on www.jasons.com

Classic Tramping in New Zealand by Shaun Barnett and Rob Brown (Craig Potton Publishing, 1999)

Accessible Walks by Anna Jameson and Andrew Jameson (Madyeti Publications, 2000)

Exploring North Island Volcanoes by Glenys Robertson (New Holland Publishers, 2005)

Tongariro National Park

Location: central North Island
Features: volcanic mountains and landscapes ■ New Zealand's
first national park ■ world's first dual natural and
cultural World Heritage Area
Activities: short walks ■ tramping ■ climbing ■ skiing and
snowboarding

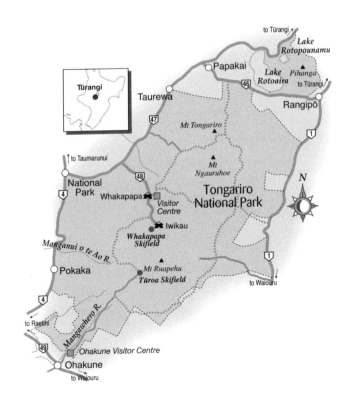

Active volcanoes, snow-covered mountain peaks, a diversity of volcanic, alpine and desert landscapes, beech and podocarp forests, lakes and waterfalls are the features that distinguish Tongariro, New Zealand's oldest national park.

The mountains Tongariro, Ngauruhoe and Ruapehu form the nucleus of the park. They can be seen for miles around, dominating the otherwise rural and forested landscape of the central North Island. There is a powerful Māori spiritual association with these mountains. In 1887 local Tūwharetoa chief Horonuku te Heuheu Tukino IV gifted the sacred peaks to the Crown, to prevent them from falling into private ownership and to protect them in perpetuity. His gift led to the establishment of New Zealand's first – and the world's fourth – national park.

Today the mountains, with their climbing opportunities, ski fields, tramping tracks and short walks attract more visitors to Tongariro than any other national park in New Zealand.

About the park

Tongariro National Park sits restlessly at the southern end of the 'Pacific Ring of Fire', a volatile expanse of volcanic and earthquake activity which emanates from tectonic movement along the rim of the Pacific crustal plate.

The park's highest volcano, Ruapehu (2797 m), dominates the surrounding countryside and is the only North Island mountain with glaciers (albeit small ones). Ruapehu's volatile, steaming crater lake is one of the few hot crater lakes in the world to be surrounded by snowfields. From time to time Ruapehu erupts. As recently as 1996 massive showers of ash, rock and steam were blasted hundreds of metres from the crater lake, and boiling lahars (rivers of mud and water) streamed down the mountain slopes.

Tongariro (1968 m) may be lower than Ruapehu but its huge massif extends over 18 km in length and has craters, steaming fumaroles, geothermal springs and volcanic vents, one of which is in fact the higher, classical cone-shaped Ngauruhoe (2291 m).

While these three volcanoes dominate the park, smaller volcanoes such as Hauhungatahi, Pihanga and Kākaramea are dotted around the park's extremities. However, by far the biggest volcanic effect on the region's landscape resulted from an eruption further afield. A huge explosion around 1800 years ago, from an immense crater now filled by Lake Taupō, is reputedly the biggest volcanic eruption to have occurred on the planet in the past 5000 years. The cataclysmic blast devastated surrounding forests and blanketed much of the North Island with pumice and ash.

Flora and fauna

The forests have recovered since the Taupō eruption and now cover Tongariro National Park's lower slopes. In the southern part of the park there is a remnant stand of podocarp forest that was sheltered from the eruption by Mt Ruapehu. Here, ancient rimu, miro and matai trees tower over a tangled profusion of understorey trees, shrubs and vines.

Younger podocarp and broadleaf forests grow at the edges of the park while, at higher altitudes, beech forest dominates. This in turn gives way to tussocklands, subalpine shrubs, wetlands and bogs, and, on the highest slopes, huge areas of lava rock and gravel that are devoid of any plant life except for the hardiest alpine herbs and mosses. In the east of the park sprawls a vast area known as the Rangipō Desert, where altitude and westerly winds have prevented post-Taupō eruption forest recovery. Growing throughout these diverse landscapes are more than 550 species of native plants, most of which are endemic to New Zealand.

The park's forests, open areas, rivers and lakes provide habitats for many native birds, including threatened species such as the brown kiwi, blue duck, New Zealand falcon, kākā, North Island robin, fernbird and long-tailed cuckoo. New Zealand's only native land mammals – short-tailed and long-tailed bats – are also present.

People in the park

The traditions of Ngāti Tūwharetoa, the Māori people who have lived in the region for over 800 years, are woven around the volcanism in the park and show the depth of Tūwharetoa understanding of the geological formations of the Tongariro region.

There is the story of the high priest Ngātoroirangi, who first explored this area to claim it for his people. When Ngātoroirangi spied a challenger for the land he called for help from his gods, who sent dark clouds and snow. Later, when Ngātoroirangi neared the summit of Tongariro he was frozen in a snowstorm and called to Hawaiki, his traditional Polynesian homeland, for warmth. Fire duly arrived via the underground passage – known today as the Pacific Ring of Fire – and erupted from a crater at the summit. This tenuous juxtaposition of fire and ice is one of the special features of Tongariro.

The park is also the birthplace of rivers with strong Māori spiritual associations, such as the Whanganui, lifeblood of the people from Te Āti Haunui a Pāpārangi. Tradition relates how the Whanganui's course was gouged by the personified mountain Taranaki as he fled from the central North Island after losing 'a mighty battle with the venerable old Tongariro over the love of the fair mountain maiden Pihanga'. Tongariro is said to have been considerably lowered in height after this battle – a reference to the immense size of Tongariro before major eruptions.

While the Tūwharetoa triple-summit gift to the Crown protected the mountains' sacredness, the creation of Tongariro National Park also cleared the way for the protection of lower altitude forests from milling when European settlers arrived to farm the land. Tourism soon became a major activity in the park: huts were built for trampers, in 1913 the first skiing pioneers explored the Whakapapa slopes and in 1929 the imposing hotel now known as the Chateau Tongariro was built at the base of Ruapehu.

Today the park hosts nearly a million visitors each year. Major drawcards are the two commercial ski areas and their associated lodges and cafés, the tramping tracks and a network of shorter walks.

The gift

Ko Tongariro te maunga, ko Taupō te awa, ko Tūwharetoa te iwi, ko te Heuheu te tangata.
Tongariro is the mountain, Taupō is the lake, Tūwharetoa is the tribe, te Heuheu is the man.

The Māori people's association with their lands, mountains, rivers and lakes is of special significance. For each tribe there is a mountain that is sacred, revered as an ancestor who represents the tribe's identity, mana (strength and prestige) and spirituality. For Tūwharetoa, that mountain is Tongariro. For the neighbouring Ngā ti Rangi and Te Āti Haunui a Pāpārangi tribes it is Ruapehu.

In the late 19th century there was fierce contention over land in the central North Island, with pressures from farming and logging settlers and rival tribes. When the government land court convened to settle these disputes and grant land titles, Tūwharetoa chief Horonuku te Heuheu Tukino IV was anguished. 'If our mountains of Tongariro are included in the blocks passed through the court in the ordinary way, what will become of them? They will be cut up and sold, a piece going to one Pakeha and a piece to another. Tongariro is my ancestor, my tupuna; it is my head; my mana centres round Tongariro; my father's bones lie there today. I cannot consent to the court passing these mountains through in the ordinary way.'

In 1885 te Heuheu gifted Tongariro, Ngauruhoe and Ruapehu to the Crown to preserve them for the people of New Zealand and in 1894 Tongariro National Park was established. The park has since grown to over three times the size of te Heuheu's original gift, thus protecting some 79,000 ha. The connection between Ngāti Tūwharetoa and the mountains was recognised internationally in 1993 when Tongariro National Park became the first dual natural and cultural World Heritage Area.

What to do

Short walks

The following is a selection of the many top-quality walks that explore a range of landscapes and are suitable for a variety of ages and fitness levels. Park brochures contain a full list of short walks.

Taranaki Falls (Whakapapa Village) 2 hours loop

A 6 km loop across tussock and subalpine shrublands, through beech forest and over lava flows, with mountain views. The falls plunge off a huge lava flow that erupted from Ruapehu some 15,000 years ago.

Silica Rapids (Whakapapa Village) 2.5 hours loop

A full range of vegetation – subalpine plants, beech forest, tussock and swampy clearings feature on this walk. It climbs gently beside a cascading headwater stream to the creamy white and red, mineral-coloured Silica Rapids. There are great views of Ruapehu and Ngauruhoe.

Meads Wall Walk (Whakapapa Ski Area) 10 minutes one way

A summertime stroll through volcanic and cinematic history. The park, in particular the Whakapapa Ski Area and Meads Wall, was a filming location for the Lord of the Rings trilogy. The jagged volcanic rocks, cliffs and barren landscape were ideally suited to create vivid scenes of Mordor, Emyn Muil and Mt Doom. The short walk leads up a rocky bluff to a stunning viewpoint.

Rotopounamu (11 km from Tūrangi) 20 minutes one way

Rotopounamu, meaning 'greenstone lake', nestles in a basin beneath Mt Pihanga, its rippling waters reflecting the rich greens of the surrounding forest. Swimming (in summer), birdwatching, or simply enjoying the delightful setting make this one of the park's most popular walks. The pleasure can be extended by walking all the way around the lake, taking the trip time to 2 hours.

Rimu Walk (Ohakune) 15 minutes loop

Short but impressive, beneath giant podocarp trees that have survived the fury of Ruapehu eruptions. The track surface is suitable for wheelchairs and strollers.

Longer walks

While the following options are part of multi-day tramping routes, they are also accessible for day trips.

Old Waihōhonu Hut (Desert Road) 3 hours return

This hut was built in 1903 as overnight accommodation for stagecoach passengers. Although is it no longer in use, it is preserved as a Historic Places Trust building. The gently graded walk (6.3 km return) meanders through open tussock country, beech forest and across a mountain stream.

Tama Lakes (Whakapapa Village) 5 to 6 hours return

Stark volcanic landscape in the broad saddle between Ruapehu and Ngauruhoe, featuring two old, water-filled explosion craters. From Whakapapa the 14 km walk continues beyond Taranaki Falls, climbs through tussock country and alpine herbfields to the signposted turn-off to the two lakes. Note that this track can be exposed to high winds and cloud cover, and is likely to be snow-covered in winter.

Tongariro Crossing (Mangatepopo Road) 7 to 8 hours one way

A strenuous climb over the lunar-like terrain between Tongariro and Ngauruhoe. This popular, sometimes crowded walk's billing as the country's finest one-day walk is deceptive, leading people to underestimate the risks involved. The 17 km route crosses high and exposed mountain country that can be subject to severe winds, white-outs and sudden storms. In winter it is snow-covered and should not be undertaken without mountaineering experience and equipment. Nevertheless, on a fine summer's day the climb over mountain saddles

Top tips

- Summer in the park has its own special appeal. Take a stroll on one of the tracks around Whakapapa Village. You don't have to be able to walk far to enjoy the park's wonderful diversity of landscapes.
- If you're travelling with stroller or wheelchair Whakapapa Nature Walk and Ohakune's Rimu Walk have sealed surfaces. Walks requiring only a little more agility are Mangawhero Falls (Ohakune) and Mounds Walk (Whakapapa).
- Rainy day? Check out the Whakapapa Visitor Centre. Through audiovisual and interactive displays you will learn all about the park, its fiery volcanic history, natural heritage and special connection with Ngāti Tūwharetoa.
- After a day in the park, call in to the salubrious Chateau Tongariro lounge for a hot chocolate or cocktail. Savour the old-world ambience – and the view of Mt Ngauruhoe framed by a picture window. It is a long-standing tradition that everyone, non-guests included, is welcome here.
- Join the Tongariro Natural History Society. Members work with park staff on special projects and promote wider understanding of the park through publications, guided walks and other activities.

and moraine walls, across volcanic craters and past steaming vents, hot springs and emerald and green lakes is a stunner – if you don't mind the crowds of fellow walkers, that is.

It is not a round trip so transport will need to be organised. Several local operators provide a shuttle service. Before setting out check the weather conditions and, even if they are excellent, take appropriate, windproof clothing in case of sudden changes. Note that the Ketetahi hot springs, on the mid slopes of Tongariro, are located in a private enclave of land.

Whakapapaiti Valley (Whakapapa) 4 to 5 hours one way

A fine mountain walk, starting above bushline, crossing rocky scoria flats and subalpine shrublands, descending alongside the pretty Whakapapaiti headwaters and returning through beech forest.

Start on the Bruce Road 5 km above Whakapapa Village and finish at Whakapapa Village. The 11 km walk involves fording the Whakapapaiti River, which might not be possible after heavy rain. Be sure to check first at the visitor centre. You will need to have a car at each end of the track or walk 5 km along the Bruce Road.

Lake Surprise (Ohakune Mountain Road) 5 hours return

A walk above bushline around the mid slopes of Ruapehu, taking in silica-coloured cascades on the Mangaturuturu River, waterfalls, bluffs and the tussock-surrounded Lake Surprise. This 9 km return walk involves some reasonably strenuous descents and climbs, plus a river to ford, where damaged vegetation shows the path of a lahar that swept through here in 1995. It is best to walk this in summer – winter ice makes travel across the cascades treacherous.

Multi-day tramping trips

A comprehensive network of tramping tracks link with park huts. The Tongariro Northern Circuit and the Round the Mountain Track around Ruapehu are linked and have several access points so sections can be walked as day or overnight trips. The most popular walking time is December to March, when the tracks are normally clear of snow and the weather more settled. Technical snow and ice travel expertise is needed for winter journeys.

Round the Mountain 4 to 6 days

A walk around the mid slopes of Mt Ruapehu, taking in a range of landscapes that include beech forest, tussocklands, alpine herbfields, glacial river valleys and barren desert lands. There are six huts en route, and some relatively remote sections.

Tongariro Northern Circuit 2 to 3 days

This route climbs up and over the stark volcanic landscapes of Tongariro's South and Red Craters and Oturere Valley, passing through beech forest and shrublands in Waihōhonu Valley then crossing the lower Tama Saddle, between Ngauruhoe and Ruapehu.

Summit ascents

While the peaks of the park are relatively easy to access, the routes are potentially dangerous to those who are inexperienced or ill equipped for this alpine terrain. The routes are unmarked. During winter and times of snow, hazards can include ice, crevasses, waterfall holes and avalanches.

At all times of year the weather can quickly deteriorate, bringing white-outs, high winds and snow or rain. Before you start check the weather and conditions. On your climb, turn back if unsure.

Ruapehu Crater Climb (Whakapapa Ski Area) 5 hours return

Starting from the top of Knoll Ridge chairlift, there are two main routes that lead onto Dome Ridge, and from there to Dome Shelter and a view of the mountain's Crater Lake. At the time of writing, the last eruption here was in 1996. Note that this is a high alpine environment, with no marked tracks, where weather can change suddenly bringing white-outs, gales, rain and snow. If inexperienced, or in doubt, guided trips are offered during summer months. Note also that the chairlift might be operating, even if the weather is unsuitable for travelling further up the mountain. The return trip from the top of the chairlift is about 7 km.

Ngauruhoe (Mangatepopo Road) 6 to 7 hours return

The almost perfectly cone-shaped Ngauruhoe, which is a massive vent of the Tongariro volcano, is a steep but popular summer climb. From Mangatepopo Road the approach walk follows the Tongariro Crossing route as far as the saddle between Ngauruhoe and Tongariro. From here the route is unmarked and very steep, climbing over slippery scoria rock directly to the summit. Do not descend into the steep crater, where volcanic gases are sometimes present. Return to the saddle via the loose scree slope – enjoy the slide, but do take care. The walk is 19 km return from the Mangatepopo roadend.

Tongariro (Red Crater) 2 hours return
Part way along the Tongariro Crossing, a poled route turns off from Red Crater and leads to the Tongariro summit. When there is no snow and the weather is good, this is a straightforward route.

Mountaineering
There are a number of short but interesting climbs on the mountains of the park, in particular on Ruapehu. The peaks around the crater rim – Tahurangi, Paretetaitonga, Te Heuheu and Girdlestone – offer routes that range from challenging to easy and suitable for beginners (with appropriate equipment and guidance of course). The Pinnacles, beside the Whakapapa Ski Area, present some challenging winter ice and snow climbs. A winter climb of the symmetrical Ngauruhoe is especially alluring, though often icy and suitable only for experienced mountaineers.

Rock climbing
For experienced and equipped climbers there is traditional rock climbing on lava bluffs both in Mangatepopo Valley and at the Whakapapa Ski Area.

Skiing
Mt Ruapehu has two of the largest skiing and snowboarding areas in the country, Whakapapa and Tūroa, which are privately operated and

offer downhill runs over a vast 1800 ha. The areas provide high-class facilities and trails ranging from easy to advanced, and are usually open from late June to mid November. Occasionally, good skiing is still possible at Christmas.

If you have suitable experience and it's a clear day it's possible to carry your skis or board beyond the lifts to the Crater Lake then enjoy a 700 m drop in altitude back to the car park. There are also some interesting off-piste runs. In good snow conditions there are ski touring opportunities around the summits of Ruapehu and Tongariro.

Hunting

Introduced red deer, sika deer and low numbers of pigs live in the park. Hunting permits are available from park offices.

Mountain biking

Although biking is not permitted in the park unless on a formed road, there are good mountain-biking opportunities on old logging roads in forests next to the park, in the Rangataua Conservation Area, Erua Forest and Tongariro Forest. Details are available at visitor centres.

Information

Getting there: The nearest towns are Tūrangi, Ohakune and National Park. There are several entry points to the park, the major one being Whakapapa Village, 1 hour's drive from Tūrangi. State Highways (SH) 1, 4, 49 and 47 lead to park entrance points. The main trunk railway stops at Ohakune and National Park. By air, the closest airport is Taupō, about 1.5 hour's drive north of the park. There are daily bus services to

Tūrangi, National Park and Ohakune, and from Tūrangi to Whakapapa Village. Two roads, Ohakune Mountain Road and Bruce Road, climb high into the park but are sometimes closed in winter because of snow. During summer several transport companies provide shuttle services to road-ends and track entrances.

When to go: Any time of the year, depending on which recreational pursuit you seek – summer for tramping and seeing alpine flowers, winter for skiing and climbing, year-round for short walks and landscape appreciation.

Climate: There are huge seasonal variations, and even within seasons the weather is unpredictable. Summer days (January to March) can be very hot but conditions can quickly change to cold temperatures, rain and possibly even snow, especially at high altitudes. Winters are cold: expect snow and frost. Rain falls year-round.

Accommodation and facilities: There are hotels, lodges, motels and camping accommodation, plus shops and restaurants in Tūrangi, Ohakune and, to a lesser extent, National Park. At Whakapapa Village accommodation includes the Chateau Tongariro (four-star hotel), motels, cabins and a campground.

Within the park there are nine huts and several camping areas, with minimal facilities such as toilets and water. Mangawhero (2 km from the Ohakune Visitor Centre) and Mangahuia Campsite (off SH47, near Whakapapa) are accessible by vehicles. Campsites are located near each of the huts on the Tongariro Northern Circuit. Hut passes and camping fees are cheaper if prepurchased. During the Great Walks season (October to June) huts on the Tongariro Northern Circuit (Mangatepopo, Ketetahi, Oturere and Waihōhonu) have resident wardens and gas cookers.

Commercial ventures: Guided walks and climbs, scenic flights, two ski areas (lift facilities, ski schools, ski hire, cafés and restaurants). Specialist climbing and tramping gear is also available for hire.

Further reading: *The Restless Land: Stories of Tongariro National Park World Heritage Area*, Department of Conservation and Tongariro Natural History Society; Tongariro Parkmap; NZMS 260 series topographical maps T20, T19, S19, S20; park brochures and fact sheets.

Special conditions: While years can pass with no volcanic rumblings, eruptions and lahars can happen at any time, with little or no warning. Anyone intending to venture onto the upper slopes should first check the volcanic alert status and follow recommended safety measures.

A sophisticated monitoring system has been installed on Ruapehu to provide early warning of the occurrence of an eruption or lahar. In the event of sudden volcanic activity skiers and trampers should move out of valleys and onto ridgelines to avoid lahar danger. Eruptions can be spectacular when viewed from a safe distance but extremely dangerous for those who venture too close.

Visitor centres: Whakapapa Visitor Centre has extensive displays and audiovisual presentations, sells books, maps, cards, souvenirs, hut passes and brochures, and can provide current information on weather, snow conditions, volcanic activity and tracks. There is a smaller park visitor centre at Ohakune and a Department of Conservation office at Tūrangi.

Whakapapa Visitor Centre
Whakapapa Village
Private Bag, Mt Ruapehu 2650
Phone 0-7-892 3729
Email whakapapavc@doc.govt.nz
Open daily 8 am to 5 pm (winter)
or 6 pm (summer)

Ohakune Visitor Centre
Mountain Road
PO Box 10
Ohakune
Phone 0-6-385 0010
Email ohakunevc@doc.govt.nz
Open Monday to Friday 9 am to 3 pm, plus weekends during school holidays

Taupō Tongariro Conservancy
Turanga Place
Private Bag
Tūrangi
Phone 0-7-386 8607
Email ttcinfo@doc.govt.nz
Open Monday to Friday 8 am to 4.30 pm

Te Urewera National Park

Location: mid-eastern North Island

Features: remote, forest-covered mountain ranges ■ lakes ■ rivers
■ waterfalls ■ history

Activities: short walks ■ tramping ■ boating ■ river kayaking
■ fishing ■ hunting

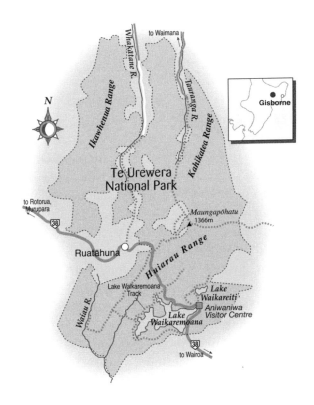

Te Urewera National Park, deep in the hinterland of the North Island's east coast, is part of the single largest tract of native forest remaining in the North Island. Because of its size and range of natural habitats, the park supports a huge diversity of native plants and wildlife, as comprehensive and intact as any left on the New Zealand mainland. In human terms, Te Urewera is filled with the presence of Ngāi Tūhoe, the tangata whenua (people of the land).

Despite the isolation – just one long and winding road penetrates the heart of the park – one of New Zealand's popular Great Walks is the Lake Waikaremoana Track. The magnificent Waikaremoana, the smaller Lake Waikareiti and a range of delightful forest walks have traditionally attracted many holidaying New Zealanders to this area of the park. In northern Te Urewera the park's main river valleys, Whaka-tāne and Tauranga, are drawcards for tramping, hunting and fishing. Other rugged, challenging tramping trips follow valleys, ridgelines and old Tūhoe trails through even more remote regions.

About the park

There is a strong essence of Māori history and spirituality in Te Urewera. Tūhoe names for landscape features, settlement sites and sacred places throughout the park reflect a tribal association with the land that goes back many centuries.

Tūhoe also have a notable tradition of resistance to European influences. In 1906 the charismatic religious leader Rua Kenana established a settlement independent of the European world at Maungapōhatu, deep in the heart of Te Urewera. Today Maungapōhatu, at the foot of the sacred Mt Maungapōhatu, remains a Tūhoe-owned enclave within the park.

Tūhoe's refusal to allow prospectors and surveyors into Te Urewera – at a time when logging and farming were destroying forests throughout New Zealand – meant the natural integrity of the region was retained.

Conservationists' moves to protect this large tract of forest led to negotiations with the Tūhoe people and, in 1954, the national park was created. Since then significant additions have been made to the park.

Ngāti Ruapani, a tribe with strong Tūhoe links, has connections in the Lake Waikaremoana region, and there is also some influence from Ngāti Kahungunu, a major tribe of the eastern regions.

Forested ranges

Te Urewera's jumbled mass of ranges reaches a maximum height of just 1392 m. The dominant Huiarau and Ikawhenua Ranges are made up of ancient, uplifted greywacke rock. To the south, younger sandstones overlaid by softer mudstones have created waterfalls and steep bluffs.

Several layers of ash, thrown from eruptions from the central North Island volcanoes, cover the entire park and form the fertile base for Te Urewera's unbroken mantle of forest. A feature of the park is the almost total lack of clear areas, even on summit ridges. These misty, cloudy places are covered with tangled, gnarled and lichen-covered silver beech forests, mixed with some mountain beech in drier places. Below about 900 m red beech and rimu dominate, while lower still northern rātā, rimu, tawa and kāmahi are the main big trees.

The forest contains more than 650 species of native plants, including many rare or vulnerable ones. For example, Te Urewera is one of the few places where kakabeak grows in the wild. This red-flowering *Clianthus puniceus* is easily cultivated but now rarely found in natural areas.

Wildlife

Te Urewera supports a collection of wildlife as comprehensive as any left on the New Zealand mainland. Nearly all the native birds present in North Island forests live in Te Urewera, including several threatened species – brown kiwi, blue duck, kākāriki, North Island kāka, New Zealand falcon and kōkako.

Other interesting fauna in the park include short-tailed and long-tailed bats, giant land snails and an as yet unnamed tusked wētā. The wētā is an ancient species from the same order as grasshoppers and crickets, and the tusked wētā (only the males have tusks) was only discovered in the 1970s. At least nine species of native fishes live in the rivers and lakes.

The lake

Lake Waikaremoana is a gem in the heart of Te Urewera, a major focus for recreation that is steeped in tradition. The name Waikaremoana means 'sea of dashing waters'. According to Tūhoe tradition this name refers to the actions of Haumapuhia, the daughter of an ancestral chief, who gouged the furrows and channels of the lake during a struggle with her father. Haumapuhia is said to have turned to stone in a narrow gorge nearby, blocking a stream which filled the channels she had gouged, and thus created the lake.

Scientific opinion would explain that Lake Waikaremoana was formed about 2200 years ago, when a massive landslide dammed a gorge of the Waikaretāheke River. Ever since, the ongoing process of erosion has continued to mould the surrounding hills and valleys. Today the immense 5439 ha lake is popular for boating, kayaking, fishing (for introduced trout) and of course for the Great Walk that follows most of the lake's perimeter, with its beech forests and splendid outlooks. The park's historic visitor centre and museum at Aniwaniwa is a special feature.

Nestling in a smaller basin 300 m above Waikaremoana is a smaller but no less beautiful 'gem', Lake Waikareiti. There are six islands in this lake, which is one of the few in the North Island free of introduced aquatic plant life, and on the largest island there is yet another lake. While beech forest covers the basin surrounding Waikareiti, plants normally associated with subalpine areas and South Island pākihi swamps grow in the nearby clearings and wetlands, making up an area known locally as 'the tundra'.

What to do

Short walks

Following is a small selection of the many short walks in the park. Most are in the vicinity of Lake Waikaremoana and Aniwaniwa Visitor Centre, while others leave from the road to Wairoa and, in the west of the park, from the road to Rotorua. A park brochure provides a full list and access details.

Hinerau Walk (Aniwaniwa) 20 minutes loop

A gently graded 1.2 km loop walk that starts beside the visitor centre and follows the Aniwaniwa River, taking in the Bridal Veil Fall and two-tiered Aniwaniwa Falls. There is also a fine outlook across Lake Waikaremoana. The walk passes through a varied range of big forest trees and semi-alpine species, many of them labelled for identification. The track is named after the legendary Tūhoe princess Hinerau, who was trapped in a rocky chasm following an earthquake while she was gathering food in the forest. Her tears of despair formed Te Tangi o Hinerau (the tears of Hinerau), the lower cascade of the Aniwaniwa Falls. Hinerau was rescued by Ruapani chief Te Toru, whom she later married.

Lou's Lookout (Onepoto, near Aniwaniwa) 40 minutes return

A short walk through rock bluffs and over huge boulders to a view of Lake Waikaremoana and its spectacular Panekiri Bluff. The track climbs over the massive landslide that collapsed off Ngāmoko Peak (to the east of the lookout) 2200 years ago, forming Lake Waikaremoana. The track is named after Lou Dolman, a long-serving policeman who helped build the track in the 1960s.

Tawa Walk (Aniwaniwa) 30 minutes loop

Tawa, with its distinctive, willow-like, yellow-green foliage, is evident on this gentle walk. However, the main feature is the variously aged northern rātā vines growing over their host trees, and in particular one of the biggest known northern rātā trees in the country. Rātā begins life as an epiphytic plant, its roots reaching down the host tree's trunk in search of water and nutrients. As the rātā grows and the host tree dies, the rātā becomes a tree in its own right, often growing to a huge size. The big rātā on Tawa Track is estimated to be a thousand years old.

Black Beech Track (Aniwaniwa) 30 minutes one way

This walk follows an old roadline between the visitor centre and Lake Waikaremoana camping ground. There is also a fine view of the Home Bay (Whanganuioparua) arm of the lake, and of Panekiri Bluff.

Lake Waikareiti (Aniwaniwa) 2 hours return

Nestling in a beech-forested basin 300 m above Lake Waikaremoana is the smaller but no less beautiful Lake Waikareiti with its six islands. This 7 km walk climbs gradually to Waikareiti, passing through forests of rimu, northern rātā, tawa then red and silver beech, before returning the same way.

At the lake edge there is a day shelter, with toilets but no overnight facilities, plus dinghies and life jackets that can be hired through the Aniwaniwa Visitor Centre for lake and island explorations. On the north-western island there is a landing stage and short track to the tiny lake on the island. A tramping track continues around the lake to an 18-bunk hut on the eastern lakeshore (bookings required for overnight stays).

Armed Constabulary Redoubt (Aniwaniwa) 45 minutes return

Some controversial events in New Zealand history occurred around Lake Waikaremoana in the 1860s and 1870s, when there was a major stand-off between powerful Māori leader Te Kooti and British forces. An armed constabulary redoubt was built at Lake Kiriopukae on the burial ground of a major Māori pā (village). At its peak it had several barracks, a cookhouse and officers' quarters. Remaining today are a cemetery, historic graffiti where soldiers etched their names, and some rock works associated with the buildings and kitchen.

A museum at the Aniwaniwa Visitor Centre tells more of the story of Te Kooti. An excellent book to read on the Te Kooti saga is Maurice Shadbolt's *Season of the Jew*.

Panekiri Bluff (Aniwaniwa) 2 hours return

A steep climb through beech forest at the eastern end of the Lake Waikaremoana Great Walk to a trig, where you will be rewarded with park and lake views. A further 3 hours from the trig is Bald Knob (1155 m), the most impressive viewpoint.

Whanganui Hut (Hopuruahine) 3 hours return

An easy and pleasant lakeside walk at the western end of the Lake Waikaremoana Great Walk. Bookings are required for overnight stays.

Multi-day tramping trips

With the exception of the Lake Waikaremoana Great Walk, Lake Waikareiti–Ruapani Circuit and the Whakatāne River Valley, the tramping tracks in the park explore remote and rugged areas and require a high standard of fitness and tramping experience.

Lake Waikaremoana Track 3 to 4 days

Red and silver beech forests, montane forests, waterfalls, secluded bays and stunning views are features of the Lake Waikaremoana Track, which circles two-thirds of the lake. Bird life is abundant, most notably kākāriki, North Island kākā, New Zealand falcons and North Island robins. At night, the calls of moreporks might be heard and, at dusk, the distinctive, screeching cries of brown kiwi.

There are five park huts (each with wood-burning fire or gas heater, water supply, cooking benches and toilets) and five campsites (cooking shelters, water supply, toilets). Cooking stoves must be carried. Camping is not permitted within 500 m of the track, except at the five designated campsites. Hut and campsite passes must be prebooked.

The eastern end of the 46 km track starts at Onepoto, on SH38 about

Saving special species

The forests of Otamatuna, in the remote north of Te Urewera, resound with the deep, booming and melodious call of kōkako. In fact, these forests contain about half of the national population of the highly endangered kōkako, and numbers are growing.

The Northern Te Urewera Ecosystem Restoration Project, a programme to control animal pests such as possums, stoats and rodents, began in 1996. It has been undertaken by conservation staff to enhance the population of kōkako and other threatened species. Otamatuna is so far the largest mainland area subjected to such intensive predator control; as a result kōkako numbers have recovered dramatically. In 1994 just eight pairs were counted in Otamatuna, but 10 years later there were at least 95 pairs – and they were obviously becoming more difficult to count!

There has also been intense predator control on Lake Waikaremoana's Puketukutuku Peninsula since 1991. In this project, conservation staff and local Māori people from the Lake Waikaremoana Hapū Restoration Trust have been working together to control stoats, the main threat to kiwi chicks, as well as possums and rats. This programme is also proving highly successful. Brown kiwi numbers are increasing and, in this much more accessible region of the park, visitors are likely to hear their distinctive, repetitive calls, usually at dusk, while on the Lake Waikaremoana Track.

10 km from Aniwaniwa. The north-western end is at Hopuruahine, on SH38 16 km west of Aniwaniwa. Local companies operate shuttle buses and water taxis. Walkers can leave vehicles at Waikaremoana Motorcamp. The track is sheltered by forest for much of the way, but the lake is almost 600 m above sea level and the climate is generally cooler, wetter and more changeable. Walkers should be suitably prepared with warm clothing and wet-weather gear. A guided walk is available.

Whakatāne Valley Loop 3 to 5 days

Follows the Whakatāne, one of the park's major rivers, from Ruatāhuna (on SH38) and returns via the Waikare tributary and over a ridgeline back to the starting point. This loop passes through a mix of river landscapes, grassy flats and mānuka and tawa forest. Walking in the Whakatāne Valley is relatively straightforward, but the Waikare section involves several river crossings and is impassable when the river is in flood. Much of the way follows well-formed horse tracks, as horses have long been a mode of transport for the Tūhoe people, some of whom you are likely to meet along the way. There are enclaves of private Tūhoe land throughout the Whakatāne Valley, including most of the large clearings and regenerating mānuka forested areas. Access across these areas is permitted; camping and hunting are not. There are five park huts. Secure car parking can be arranged at Ruatāhuna.

As an alternative to the Waikare loop, it is also possible to continue down the Whakatāne Valley. A further 7 to 9 hours' walking leads to Ruatoki Road, 18 km from Taneatua and SH2.

Top tips

- Spend some time in the Aniwaniwa Visitor Centre. It's designed by well-known Māori architect John Scott, and its museum offers a look at the fascinating history of the area.
- Take a water taxi to one of the delightful bays around the Waikaremoana lakeshore and enjoy a picnic, or visit a waterfall, or walk a section of the Lake Waikaremoana Track.
- Hire a rowboat on Lake Waikareiti and explore the islands. They are covered by forest that's totally unmodified by browsing possums or deer.
- Pack a rod. Sandy Bay Hut on Lake Waikareiti is a great base for fishing on the lake.
- Onepoto Caves are well worth an exploration. There's historical and geological interest, good fun and great views.

Lake Waikareiti–Ruapani Circuit 1 to 2 days

A delightful medley of differing forest types, lakes, wetlands and abundant bird life. Follow the walking path from Aniwaniwa to the Lake Waikareiti shelter, then continue on a walking track to the head of the lake and Sandy Bay Hut. Enjoy its white, sandy beach. Return the way you came to the north-west corner of the lake, then branch right onto Ruapani Track. This brings you back to your starting point at Aniwaniwa, along the way passing several wetland basins and Lake Ruapani. Kākā, kākāriki, robins and riflemen frequent these areas, and tall kahikatea trees thrive in the swampy conditions. There are good views from Ruapani Track of Lake Waikaremoana, Mt Manuoha (at 1392 m the highest point in the park), and the Ngāmoko Range.

Options on this circuit include hiring a rowboat to cross Lake Waikareiti to Sandy Bay Hut. Bookings are essential for this hut.

Lake Waikareiti–Manuoha Track 3 to 4 days

A challenging 32 km trip for experienced trampers that takes in Mt Manuoha, an unusual 'tundra' area of subalpine wetland vegetation and pretty Lake Waikareiti. The track can be walked in either direction, from Aniwaniwa or Waitukupuna Bridge on SH38, 16 km west of Aniwaniwa. There are two huts. The first, Manuoha, sits 100 m above the treeline on Mt Manuoha. Views from the high point extend as far as the Tongariro mountains. The track passes through tall red beech, and moss- and lichen-covered silver and mountain beech. Close to Sandy Bay Hut is Kaipo Lagoon, where plants normally associated with subalpine areas and South Island pākihi swamps grow.

Bookings are essential for Sandy Bay Hut. There is no water along the Mt Manuoha to Sandy Bay Hut section. Walkers should be of good fitness and well prepared for weather changes, including snow. The track is actually a route – it is reasonably rough but well marked.

Waiau Valley to Lake Waikaremoana 3 to 5 days

A remote and rugged route through magnificent beech and podocarp forests and wilderness rivers. It involves many river crossings or longer and steeper all-weather routes. There are five huts but at least one night of camping is necessary. This trip starts on SH38, 7 km west of Ruatāhuna. At the Waikaremoana end trampers can join the Lake Waikaremoana Great Walk at Maraunui Bay (near Marauiti Hut), or continue along the ridge then descend to Hopuruahine Landing, at the end of the Lake Waikaremoana Great Walk, or to SH38 at Tāupeupe Saddle, 10 km from Hopuruahine Landing.

Caving

The Onepoto (Te-Ana-o-Tawa) Caves, just 10 km south of Aniwaniwa, are well worth exploring. Geological history tells that these caves were formed by the same major earthquake that created Lake Waikaremoana. Huge blocks of layered sandstone fractured and bent as they fell, creating a jigsaw of interlocking rocks with narrow tunnels and caves between and beneath them. The caves are a well-known part of Ngāti Ruapani lore. They are known as a place of shelter, and as the spot where chief Tuai fought against opposing Kahungunu warriors.

A short walk, a torch and extreme care in the dark caverns are all that's required to explore these caves. A 10-minute approach leads to the caves, where short tracks explore rock overhangs and tunnels up to 20 m long, some with multiple entrances. Cave wētā and glow worms live in some of the caves. There are also excellent viewpoints overlooking the cave system and Lake Waikaremoana. Beware of deep holes and slippery surfaces. Children should be watched carefully.

Boating

Lake Waikaremoana is a traditional boating playground, be it by power boat, yacht or kayak. It is also used for fishing or access to picnic, camping and walking spots in any of the lake's sheltered bays. Jet skis and float planes are not permitted on the lake, and boaties are warned that lake conditions can change rapidly. Remember the Māori translation of Waikaremoana – 'sea of dashing waters'.

Fishing

Introduced brown and rainbow trout are present in Lakes Waikare-moana and Waikareiti and many of the rivers. Lake Waikaremoana has no closed season. Fishing licences are are available from the Waikaremoana Motorcamp or online at www.fishandgame.org.nz.

Hunting

Recreational hunting for introduced red deer, pigs and a small herd of rusa deer is encouraged in the park. Hunting in the catchments of Waikaremoana and Waikareiti is not permitted from 20 December to 31 January. Hunting permits are available from park visitor centres or Department of Conservation offices.

Information

Getting there: The nearest towns are Rotorua, Murupara and Ruatāhuna to the west, Whakatāne and Taneatua to the north, and Wairoa to the east. The park is linked to the outside world by SH38, a winding, partly unsealed road that traverses the heart of the park between Lake Waikaremoana and Murupara.

From Rotorua, follow SH5, turn left onto SH38 at Rainbow Mountain. The road passes Murupara and continues to Lake Waikaremoana and Wairoa. From Whakatāne, roads turn off SH2 to the northern valleys. Shuttle bus and water taxi transport for trampers is available.

When to go: Any time, though summer is warmer and more settled.

Climate: Rainfall (2500 mm annually) is higher than on the surrounding lowlands. Summers are warm and drier. There are frequent frosts in winter and snow often falls below 1000 m. There can be strong winds in high places. Mist, fog and low cloud are common.

Accommodation and facilities: In the small settlement of Aniwaniwa, Waikaremoana Motorcamp offers motels, cabins, tent sites, petrol and a store. A variety of accommodation is available in the towns near the park. There is accommodation and a café/restaurant at Big Bush Holiday Park, 10 minutes from the eastern boundary near Tuai village, and Whakamarino Lodge at Tuai, 15 minutes from the park boundary. There are three park campsites alongside SH38, at Mōkau (self-registration, 8 km from Aniwaniwa), Taita-a-Makoro (free, 20 km from Aniwaniwa) and Orangihīkoia (free, 25 km from Aniwaniwa).

Commercial ventures: Water taxis, shuttle transport, guided walking, fishing and hunting, helicopter hunting and fishing access, scenic flights. Kayaks and dinghies can be hired at Waikaremoana Motorcamp.

Further reading: Te Urewera Parkmap; NZMS 260 series topographical maps V16, V17, V18, W16, W17, W18; Terramap Waikaremoana and Whirinaki; park brochures and fact sheets; *Season of the Jew*, Maurice Shadbolt; *Gilbert Mair: Te Kooti's Nemesis*, Ron Crosby.

Special conditions: If tramping in the park, good footwear (boots), strong pack, wet-weather gear and warm thermal clothing are essential. The weather is highly unpredictable, even in summer. Before leaving on a trip check the weather forecast but be aware conditions can change rapidly. Snow has been known to fall in December.

Respect enclaves of private land in the park.

Visitor centres: Aniwaniwa Visitor Centre offers information and advice on park activities and weather, and sells hut tickets, hunting permits, Lake Waikareiti rowboat hire, maps and brochures. There is also a Department of Conservation visitor centre at Murupara, near the western entrance to the park.

Aniwaniwa Visitor Centre
Aniwaniwa
Private Bag 2213, Wairoa
Phone 0-6-837 3803
Email urewerainfo@doc.govt.nz
Open daily 8 am to 4.45 pm

Rangitīkei Visitor Centre
State Highway 38
Murupara
Phone 0-7-366 1082
Open daily 8 am to 5 pm (summer);
Monday to Friday (winter)

Taranaki–Egmont National Park

Location: west coast of the North Island

Features: classic, cone-shaped volcanic mountain ■ volcanic landforms ■ subalpine shrublands ■ rainforest ■ wetlands ■ streams and waterfalls

Activities: short walks ■ tramping ■ mountaineering ■ rock climbing

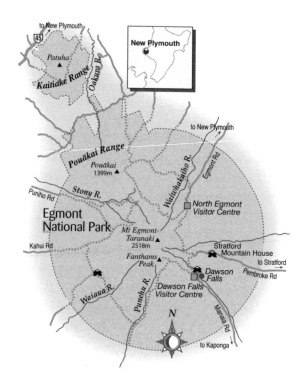

Taranaki, also known as Mt Egmont, dominates the landscape, the weather, the history and the economy of Taranaki province. The cone-shaped volcano, an imposing sentinel that stands in splendid isolation on the westernmost tip of the North Island, is also the dominating feature – the *raison d'être* in fact – of the park.

New Zealand's second oldest national park, Egmont was created in 1900 to safeguard the mountain's natural integrity and the great outdoor playground that was, even then, popular with local people. Mountaineering, rock climbing, tramping, skiing on a small club field and short forest walks featuring deep pools, cascading waterfalls, 'goblin forest' and great mountain views have been popular activities for generations. Today nearly 400,000 visitors from all over the world arrive each year to experience and explore the mountain landscapes and diversity of forest types found on and around Taranaki, the second highest mountain in the North Island.

About the park

From a distance the park looks simple: a volcano blanketed with snow in winter and flanked by green forest. Look closer, or try walking up, down or around the mountain tracks and a very different picture emerges.

The composition of that perfect-looking mountain is the result of thousands of years of powerful natural forces – volcanic build-up and weathering erosion. There are streams, rivers, lakes and swamps, immense lava bluffs, deep gorges, waterfalls and unstable slips. The summit is a world of rock, ice, moss and lichen. The upper slopes are covered with tussock, subalpine shrubs and flowers. Descending further, there are wind-blown mountain cedar forests while in the lower regions dense forests of kāmahi, northern rātā and rimu are festooned with epiphytes, filled with ferns, vines and smaller trees, and echo with native birdsong. And even that is very much a simplification of the varied and complex ecosystems found throughout the park.

The mountain

Taranaki is the Māori name for the mountain. This was unknown to British explorer Lieutenant James Cook when he sailed along the coastline in 1770 and called the volcano Egmont, after the First Lord of the Admiralty. Today, either name is accepted for the mountain, although the national park has, for now, kept just the English name.

The mountain is the most recent of a chain of andesitic volcanoes in the region to have erupted over the past two million years. To the north the older, eroded volcanoes of Pouākai and Kaitake also lie within the park, adding significantly to the variation of landscapes and disrupting that otherwise perfectly circular boundary.

As the Taranaki volcano built up in a series of violent eruptions of lava and tephra over several thousand years, debris mantled the surrounding land and laid a fertile foundation for what is now an intensive regional farming industry. The mountain has erupted eight times in the last 500 years, the last blast of ash occurring in 1775. Although Taranaki is often described as dormant, few geologists consider its volcanic life is finished. Both scientific experts and Māori elders believe that, one day, the mountain may again erupt in violent upheaval.

Taranaki is a symbol of great power to the many Māori tribes that have lived around the mountain since about the 14th century. These people have their own way of describing the volcano's arrival. According to their story, Taranaki once lived among the other mountain 'gods' of the central North Island. He fled to his present location following a battle with the mighty Tongariro over the love of Pihanga. As he fled, Taranaki gouged the bed of the Whanganui River. Taranaki's summit, or head, is a sacred place. Māori describe the summit rocks and ice as Taranaki's skull, the low-growing subalpine shrubs are his hair, the hardened lava ridges his bones, the rivers and streams his life-giving veins, and the mantle of forest his cloak.

The park has an extremely high rainfall. Taranaki acts as a magnet to passing weather systems, and as moisture-laden winds meet the mountain they are forced to rise. They cool, then deposit rain. At higher, cooler altitudes, this often turns quickly to snow and ice. Winds, too, become strong with increasing altitude and diminishing shelter, while katabatic flows of cold air often blast down the lower valleys.

The weather can cause problems for careless trampers and climbers in the park. The incredible steepness of Taranaki and the easy accessibility from road-ends to dangerous, exposed terrain are added factors visitors must consider if they are to safely enjoy their park experience. Cold rain or snow, bad visibility, steep, slippery ice and huge bluffs are dangerous combinations! But it needn't be bad. The park also enjoys a high percentage of sunshine.

Distinctive vegetation

The vegetation here is significantly different from other parks in New Zealand. The changeable weather patterns, extreme range of altitude, and isolation from other mountains and forests have led to the growth of distinctive vegetation types. No beech forest grows here; instead the lower slopes are clothed with dense rainforest, dominated by lofty northern rātā and rimu that are festooned with a range of epiphytic plants unequalled throughout the rest of New Zealand.

Goblin forest and cloud forest are oft-used descriptions for the lichen-covered kāmahi montane forest. Higher still, from about 1000 m, the striking deep greens of mountain cedar dominate. Above the bushline there is a paucity of subalpine species compared with other North Island mountains, yet some plants that grow here are found nowhere else in New Zealand. Two endemic alpine flowers, mountain foxglove (*Ourisia macrophylla*) and Mt Egmont buttercup (*Ranunculus nivicola*), make a delightful track-side show in early summer.

Park wetlands are of particular botanical interest for the variety of plants that have adapted to these special conditions. More than 260 plant species, including some endemic varieties, grow in the Ahukawakawa Swamp between Mt Taranaki and the Pouākai Range.

A range of natural habitats supports some of New Zealand's rarer species of wildlife, such as the brown kiwi, fernbird and New Zealand falcon, plus kererū, tūī, bellbirds and North Island riflemen.

Historical snippets

While there is now no charge to enter New Zealand's national parks, it wasn't always the case here. At the North Egmont park entrance, Rahiri Cottage was built in 1929 to house the park's gatekeeper, who collected a toll for entrance to the park. Funds raised helped develop the original one-way road into the two-way, sealed highway of today. The restored cottage is used now as bed-and-breakfast accommodation.

The Camphouse, at North Egmont, is another unique accommodation option in the park. The oldest surviving building in any New Zealand national park and registered Category 1 with the New Zealand Historic Places Trust, the Camphouse used to be a military barracks in New Plymouth during the Taranaki land wars of the 1860s. The building was brought by sledge to North Egmont in 1891 and restored and upgraded in 1999. Features such as hand-wrought corrugated iron complete with gunshot scars, and tongue-and-groove timber panelling, are still visible. Today the Camphouse offers self-catering accommodation for park visitors.

What to do

Short walks

Some delightful short walks leave from the main entrances to the park, Dawson Falls, East Egmont and North Egmont. They explore a range of natural and historic features. Following is a selection of the most popular.

Wilkies Pools Loop Track (Dawson Falls) 1.5 hours return

A gentle wander through the goblin forest of tangled, stunted, lichen-covered mountain cedar, tōtara and the distinctive red, papery-barked, early-summer flowering tree fuchsia to Wilkies Pools in the Kapuni

Stream. These pools are a work of nature's art, crafted over 20,000 years by the scouring actions of waterborne sand, ash and gravels in an old lava flow. The walk continues past more water action, Twin Falls and Bubbling Springs as it completes its loop.

Dawson Falls Power Station (Dawson Falls) 20 minutes return
Some historic interest here: the hydro power station driven by the Kapuni Stream is the world's second oldest functioning power station, operating since 1896 and still providing power for Dawson Falls Tourist Lodge.

Dawson Falls (Dawson Falls) 1 hour loop
A lookout point 150 m from the road provides an impressive view of these falls, plunging 18 m off a 1800-year-old lava flow. Steps lead to the bottom of the falls and a track lined with tree fuchsias and ferns leads back to the visitor centre and car park. The falls are called Rere-a-Noke by the Māori people, after a warrior who hid from pursuers behind them.

York Loop Track (East Egmont) 3 hours loop
A heritage walk exploring an old railway and a quarry established in 1903 that during the 1940s supplied rock for building the New Plymouth–Wellington railway line. Information signs explain the workings of the old crusher site, water pipeline and small railway.

Pātea Loop Track (East Egmont) 2 hours loop
Explores dense, tangled kāmahi forest, crosses dry, stony riverbeds and climbs through montane forest featuring large mountain cedars. It returns in similar forest down the other side of Pembroke Road.

Pōtaemā Track (East Egmont) 15 to 30 minutes return
Signposted from Pembroke Road, 2 km inside the park boundary, this path leads through dense forest of rimu, northern rātā and kāmahi to a large lowland bog. Rushes, sedges and mosses grow in the boggy soil, and kahikatea thrives. There are great mountain views across the open bog. The path is suitable for wheelchairs.

Enchanted Track (East Egmont) 2 to 3 hours one way

This walk descends from the mountain end of Pembroke Road through forests of horopito, kāmahi, tōtara and astelias, demonstrating how vegetation changes with altitude. Along the way Jacksons Lookout features grand mountain views. The track comes back to Pembroke Road at Mountain House, 3 km from your starting point.

Veronica Loop Track (North Egmont) 2 hours loop

This heads up on a stepped track through stunted forest, then turns downhill and returns through changing montane and subalpine forest, featuring great summit views. Before turning down, it's well worth heading uphill a further 10 minutes to a viewing seat, where you can take in the piled remnants of an old lava flow known as Humphries Castle and, further afield, the Taranaki countryside and coastline.

Longer walks

Fanthams Peak (Dawson Falls) 5 hours return

A staunch climb that leads through changing vegetation zones then continues above the bushline. Note that this upper section is very exposed and should not be attempted in winter except by experienced parties with ice axes and crampons. During summer, beware of quickly changing weather that can obscure visibility.

The first part of the track leads through beautiful goblin forest, then continues through subalpine plants and snow tussock and onto a steep, rocky 'staircase' to join with the upper round-the-mountain circuit. From here a poled route zigzags up steep scoria slopes to the top of Fanthams Peak and Syme Hut. The views along the way are outstanding.

Lake Dive (Dawson Falls) 6 to 8 hours loop

An energetic day trip, suitable for good summer conditions, that incorporates ladders and staircases. Features are Hasties Hill, an excellent lookout, two lava domes known as the Beehives, and Lake Dive.

The trip can be a circuit using the upper and lower round-the-mountain tracks, though the upper track should not be taken in winter unless your party is experienced and equipped with ice axes and crampons.

Waingongoro Round Trip (Dawson Falls) 4 to 5 hours loop

From Dawson Falls set out on Wilkies Pools Track, then continue on the upper round-the-mountain track to Enchanted Track at the upper end of Pembroke Road, East Egmont. Descend Enchanted Track then return along Waingongoro Track (also the lower round-the-mountain track), which crosses several streams and the highest swingbridge in the park. Waingongoro Hut is down a 10-minute side track near the bridge. In good summer weather this is a delightful day trip incorporating diverse forest types, mountain views, streams, slips and subalpine landscapes. Note the upper section should not be attempted in winter, except by experienced parties with ice axes and crampons.

Multi-day tramping trips

Around the Mountain 4 to 5 days (low level) or 3 to 4 days (high level)

The low-level circuit is a traditional tramping trip in the park. The first section was cut in the 1880s, well before the national park was established. It encompasses all of the park's diverse landscape features: changing forest types, volcanic landforms, waterfalls, bluffs, gorges and mountain views. There are five huts and several access points. While the track is well defined, slips and erosion occur constantly in this volatile mountain terrain and keeping it open and well maintained is challenging and expensive. Consequently park management has in recent years concentrated on developing the Pouākai Circuit (see below).

A second, high-level round-the-mountain circuit is shorter, quite stunning in summer, but exposed to extreme weather conditions and not recommended for winter use except by experienced parties with ice axes and crampons.

Pouākai Circuit 2 to 3 days

Explores subalpine terrain with great mountain views, lava cliffs and gorges, the vast Ahukawakawa Swamp wetland, the broad tussock tops of the Pouākai Range, rivers, waterfalls and fine examples of the park's tangled, lichen-covered montane goblin forest. The 25 km circuit starts and finishes at North Egmont and can also be accessed via the Pouākai Range. Walking clockwise, the track climbs from North Egmont to above the bushline, then sidles around the mountain's mid slopes past lava cliffs, ochre-coloured headwater streams and summer-flowering alpine herbs to Holly Hut. This section climbs as high as 1300 m and is likely to be snow-covered from time to time during winter.

From Holly Hut the track crosses the vast Ahukawakawa Swamp, with all of its botanical treasures, and climbs onto the Pouākai Range to Pouākai Hut, then descends into forest and sidles around the mountain's lower slopes back to North Egmont. Most of the circuit has been developed to a high standard, except for parts of the lower forested section, which can be very muddy and involve river crossings that can be flooded during heavy rain. An alternative way out is down Mangorei Track from the Pouākai Range to the park's northern boundary. Shuttle transport is available for charter.

Mountaineering

In 1839 German geologist Ernst Dieffenbach and whaler James Heberley became the first people to climb to the Taranaki summit. After an arduous approach through dense forests, they were abandoned at the snowline by their Māori guides, who believed the summit to be tapu (sacred). Māori ask today's climbers to be respectful of this sacredness. They would prefer that nobody climb over their ancestor, but as a compromise ask that individuals show their respect by not making that last climb onto the summit rock.

Climbing the mountain has long been a popular challenge, with some local climbers counting more than a hundred ascents. Nevertheless a climb on Taranaki is not to be taken lightly. The mountain is steep and exposed to changeable, unpredictable weather, and has claimed the lives of a disproportionate number of climbers. The ease of access is an added issue, with people who are ill equipped and inexperienced in mountain conditions quickly walking higher than they can manage and getting into difficulties.

There are several climbing routes, and all require alpine experience and equipment. The main summer route follows the north-east ridge above North Egmont. Depending on fitness levels, this takes 4 to 7 hours up and 3 to 4 hours down. Mountain guides run regular summit trips, and the New Zealand Alpine Club publishes a comprehensive guide to climbing in the park.

Rock climbing

Lava crags such as Humphries Castle and Warwicks Castle offer some good rock climbing. Again, the New Zealand Alpine Club's guide to climbing in the park is the best reference.

Top tips

- Pouākai Circuit is an excellent tramping trip with lots of variety. Walk it clockwise.
- Base yourself in Holly Hut (3 hours from North Egmont) overlooking Ahukawakawa Swamp. From there you can visit Bell Falls, where water has worn its way through a dome-shaped lava rock; botanise among the park's endemic wetland and subalpine plants; or wander one of the prettiest subalpine sections of the round-the-mountain track.
- Looking for adventure? Hire a licensed mountain guide and climb to the summit.
- Sit in the sun beside Wilkies Pools, listen to the birdsong, smell the fresh dampness of the mountain bush.

Skiing

A small club field operates on Stratford Plateau, at the end of Pembroke Road, East Egmont. Non-members can buy tow passes for the day and hire equipment in New Plymouth and at the Stratford Mountain House. The club can host up to 30 ski operating days a season.

Information

Getting there: The park is within 30 minutes' drive of New Plymouth city and Stratford and Hāwera towns. There are daily air and bus services to New Plymouth. Several roads climb into the park, the three main entrance points being North Egmont (Egmont Road, near New Plymouth), East Egmont (Pembroke Road near Stratford) and Dawson Falls (Manaia Road near Hāwera). Other roads lead to more remote walking tracks. Shuttle transport is available from New Plymouth.

When to go: Summer for walks, tramping, alpine flowers (best in December and January). Winter for snow climbing.

Climate: Generally hot in summer and cold and frosty in winter. However, stormy cold weather can occur at any time of the year. Rainfall increases and temperature decreases with altitude. On the forested lower slopes the mean temperature is 14°C; at the summit it is 2°C.

Accommodation and facilities: Accommodation within the park includes tourist lodges, self-catering lodges and park huts. Bookings are essential for the park's two self-catering lodges, the Camphouse (North Egmont) and Kōnini Lodge (Dawson Falls). There is a café at the North Egmont Visitor Centre and Dawson Falls Mountain Lodge. Local towns provide a full range of services, including shops, banks, restaurants and accommodation.

Commercial ventures: Several companies offer guided walks and climbs. Climbing equipment can be hired. There are also three licensed accommodation providers and several transport operators.

Further reading: *Taranaki Mount Egmont: A Guide for Climbers,* Ross Eden (New Zealand Alpine Club); Egmont Parkmap; NZMS 260 series topographical maps P20, P19, Q20; park brochures and maps; *The Story of Egmont National Park,* Department of Conservation.

Special conditions: Be wary of sudden changes in weather, particularly on the exposed slopes above the bushline. Also be aware that steep terrain, ice and snow, requiring climbing expertise and equipment, is easily accessible from road-ends. Keep away from conditions that you can't handle.

Visitor centres: There are two visitor centres within the park, both offering information, weather and track updates, maps, brochures and hut tickets. North Egmont also has informative displays. Interpretive walks and talks with park staff can be arranged for school and special-interest groups.

Dawson Falls Visitor Centre
Manaia Road
RD29, Kaponga
Hāwera
Phone 027 433 0248
Email dawsonfallsvc@doc.govt.nz
Open daily 8 am to 4.30 pm
(school holidays) or Wednesday
to Saturday (rest of year)

North Egmont Visitor Centre
Egmont Road
RD6, Inglewood
Phone 0-6-756 0990
Email nevc@doc.govt.nz
Open daily 8 am to 4.30 pm

Whanganui National Park

Location: mid-west North Island
Features: historic and wilderness river ▪ huge area of lowland
             forest
Activities: river canoeing/kayaking and rafting ▪ jetboating
             ▪ short walks ▪ tramping ▪ scenic and historic drive

The focus of this park is the historic waterway of the Whanganui and the huge tract of forest through which the river flows for much of its 300 km journey from the central North Island mountains to the sea. The forest is the North Island's largest remaining area of native lowland forest.

A 3 to 4 day tramping track traverses the heart of this forested wilderness, along the Matemateaonga Range. Another leads through the Mangapurua Valley, where grassy flats of abandoned farms merge with regenerating native forest, and several short walks explore scenic and historic features around the margins of the park. However, it is the Whanganui River itself that is the feature 'track' of this park.

The Whanganui is the longest continuously navigable river in New Zealand. Each year many thousands of people canoe some or all of the 170 km of river that flows through the park. Nearly half of this journey passes through remote, forested wilderness. The river flows through several deep gorges yet its gradient is gentle. While there are 239 named rapids between Taumarunui and Wanganui, most have less than a metre fall and the river is known for its suitability for beginners. This river trip is known as the Whanganui Journey and is part of the Great Walks network.

About the park

Great journeys have been a feature of the Whanganui's history right from the time of the land's creation. The Māori people believe the riverbed was gouged by the mountain god Taranaki as he left his original place alongside the central North Island mountains in flight from the mighty Tongariro, after a lost battle over the love of Pihanga. After Taranaki halted his flight, on the coast north of the Whanganui, streams of water sprang from the side of Tongariro to fill and heal the wound Taranaki had made in the earth, and thus formed the Whanganui River.

Te Āti Haunui a Pāpārangi are the Māori people who have lived along the Whanganui for centuries. The river formed a natural route between the coast and the interior. Food was plentiful from both the forests and the river, and Māori lived in kāinga (villages) along its length. They travelled in waka (canoes) and built large and sophisticated utu piharau (weirs) to trap lamprey, a blind, eel-like fish that moves upstream to spawn. Today fewer Māori people live along the river. The remote middle reaches, where there is no road access, are deserted. However, spiritual links with the river remain strong. Rapids, gorges and landforms throughout the park all have names associated with Māori history. The name Whanganui refers to the big (nui) wait (whanga) of the ancestral chief, Haunui a Pāpārangi. (Wanganui, the city, is a misspelt but entrenched version of the river name.)

The river's use for transport continued with the arrival of European settlers and missionaries in the mid 19th century. Mission stations established at riverside villages still carry Māori versions of biblical names, such as Koriniti (Corinth) and Ātene (Athens).

There was some unrest along the river during a period of resistance to European settlement led by the Hauhau, the name given to followers of the Pai Marire faith, a combination of Old Testament doctrine and traditional Māori beliefs. Today Maraekōwhai Historic Reserve, beside the confluence of the Whanganui and Ōhura Rivers, is most famous for the presence of two Hauhau niu poles that were erected in the 1860s.

The first pole is Rongo Niu, the war pole, reportedly built with a spirit placed inside by a tohunga (priest) that radiated through the pole's crossarms to call warriors to resist the Europeans. The second pole is Riri Kore, the peace pole, built to counter the influence of Rongo Niu when fighting ceased along the river. River travellers are able to visit Maraekōwhai, which is managed by the Maraekōwhai Whenua Trust with assistance from the Department of Conservation.

The late 19th century saw a lively era of riverboats and tourism. Tourists travelled on a three-day cruise with overnight stays in Pipiriki House, a grand hotel which has long since burnt down, and a salubrious riverboat hotel moored upstream at Maraekōwhai from 1904 to 1927. Up to 12 vessels plied the river, the largest over 30 m long and carrying up to 400 passengers. The riverboats also provided transport for Māori people and for farmers attempting to settle areas in the remote middle reaches.

When the main trunk railway line was completed in 1908 the Whanganui's importance as a transport route diminished. Tourists were enticed to other areas, remote farms were abandoned and urban drift saw the Māori population dwindle. Today there are many historical features within or close to the park. In Wanganui city, a restored, working riverboat and a riverboat museum are the products of an enthusiastic trust. On the Whanganui River Road a restored flour mill and, in the park, the historic Mangapurua 'Bridge to Nowhere' are now visitor attractions.

River reserves were first established during the riverboat era to safeguard scenic qualities for tourism. Gradually more of the forest throughout the huge Whanganui basin became protected and, in 1986, a collection of reserves, unallocated Crown land and state forest was gathered together to become Whanganui National Park.

The river

The Whanganui River is legally not part of the park, but integrally linked to it. Its special characteristics – its often muddy appearance, fearsome floods, and deeply gouged gorges, bluffs and waterfalls that have so impressed generations of visitors – are all natural phenomena.

The river starts high on the volcanic mountains of the central North Island, but for over half its journey flows though the jumble of heavily dissected hills, ridges and valleys that make up the park. The hills are formed of sedimentary sandstones and mudstones, known locally as papa, which are soft and easily eroded by water. As erosion continues its relentless work, the landscape gains sharp-crested ridges, deep-cut gorges, sheer papa bluffs and striking waterfalls.

The maze of rivers and streams that feed the Whanganui carry huge loads of papa sediment. In times of heavy rain the Whanganui valley has witnessed some tremendous floods, which have damaged roads, park huts and campsites.

Unbroken forests

A mantle of fertile volcanic ash that overlays the Whanganui basin, combined with the moist, mild climate, has produced extensive lowland forest. Tall rewarewa, northern rātā and podocarps emerge above a uniform canopy of kāmahi, tawa, hīnau and pigeonwood trees. There is a great diversity of understorey plants, trees, shrubs and vines, while a multitude of ferns, mosses, creepers and orchids grow on the forest floor and as epiphytes in the trees. Tree ferns are a feature of the park.

The steep banks of the Whanganui, and many of its tributaries, are matted with shrubs, creeping plants, kiekie, sedges, lichens and mosses. On drier banks mountain flax, toetoe and yellow-flowering kōwhai are prominent, while on shaded, damp slopes the distinctive herb parataniwha, with its varying lime-green through to bronze-red colouring, is a feature. A continual natural cycle of growth, erosion and regrowth occurs on these papa banks; only walls that have recently slipped are completely devoid of vegetation.

Native wildlife

The Whanganui, its tributaries and the huge forest of the park support a range of native wildlife. Most common North Island native forest birds thrive. There are also significant populations of brown kiwi and North Island robins, while threatened species present are the yellow-crowned parakeet (kākāriki), North Island kākā, New Zealand falcon and whitehead. Long-tailed bats are sometimes seen at dusk.

The rare blue duck lives in some tributaries, in particular the Manganui o te Ao, which flows directly from the volcanic slopes of Mt Ruapehu and does not carry the heavy silt load of most park streams.

Native aquatic life is plentiful. Large numbers of eels live in the park's waterways until they leave for their epic, once-in-a-lifetime journey to the Pacific Ocean to spawn. In contrast, blind lamprey live in the sea then migrate up the Whanganui to spawn. Several species of galaxiid are present and freshwater crayfish live in the smaller side streams.

Above: Mt Ruapehu in World Heritage Tongariro National Park. Looking across the park's Rangipō Desert from the Desert Road. (Shaun Barnett/Black Robin Photography)

Right: Kākā. Dry tree holes make ideal nest sites for this bush parrot. (Dave Hansford)

Above: A wooden carving at Whakapapa Visitor Centre reflects the special significance of the Tongariro mountains to Ngāti Tūwharetoa. (SB) Below: Emerald Lakes, mineral-coloured water-filled explosion craters on Mt Tongariro. (SB)

Above: Mangatepopo Stream flows off the slopes of Mt Ngauruhoe. Subalpine shrub and tussocklands are typical park landscape in Tongariro. (DH) Below: Lake Waikaremoana from Panekiri Bluff, Te Urewera National Park. (SB)

Opposite top: Stunted silver beech forest on Mt Manuoha. Te Urewera National Park is part of the largest single tract of native forest remaining in the North Island. (SB)

Opposite bottom left: Tauranga River, Te Urewera. Tramping tracks follow some of the major river valleys in the park. (SB)

Opposite bottom right: Lake Waikareiti, near the Sandy Bay Hut, Te Urewera National Park. (SB)

Above: Classic, cone-shaped volcano Mt Taranaki/Egmont overlooks the botanically rich Ahukawakawa Swamp. (SB)

Right: Icy winter shelter, Syme Hut on Fanthams Peak, Egmont National Park. (SB)

Above: Pied tit, one of the friendliest, most common native birds in North Island forests. (DH)

Left: Pigeonwood berries and lichen, Egmont National Park. (Darryn Pegram/Black Robin Photography)

Opposite top: The 3 day Matemateaonga Track, in Whanganui National Park, follows the crest of the forest-covered Matemateaonga Range. (SB)

Opposite bottom: Whanganui National Park is an important stronghold of the brown kiwi. (DH)

Left: Much of the 3 to 5 day Whanganui River Journey passes through a gorged wilderness inaccessible by road. (DP)

Below: Mangapurua's 'Bridge to Nowhere' in Whanganui National Park. Built for farming settlers, now used by trampers. (DP)

What to do

Whanganui Journey 4 to 5 days

Whanganui is New Zealand's most canoed river, known for its suitability for novice canoeists or kayakers. The river's major appeal is the huge forested wilderness through which it flows, the dramatic gorges, bluffs, waterfalls and strong historic essence. Nevertheless there are 239 named rapids and, though most are of a gentle nature, some have the ability to create navigational havoc. When the river level rises, as it does frequently and quickly with heavy rainfall in the Whanganui's huge catchment, many rapids are flattened and the journey becomes faster and generally more straightforward, though strong eddies need to be watched for, and one or two notorious rapids become rather more challenging.

Although a river journey, the Whanganui is part of New Zealand's Great Walks network. It is suitable for all kinds of craft: river kayaks, open-style Canadian canoes (popular for the amount of food and equipment they can carry) or rafts, though the latter tend to be slower and harder to paddle. Some canoeists travel 145 km from Taumarunui to Pipiriki. The upper reaches near Taumarunui flow through farm and forest and have a greater concentration of rapids. A more popular, shorter, 3 day journey from Whakahoro to Pipiriki (87 km) is a true wilderness experience. This section is entirely in the park, there is no road access to the river and it traverses one of the most rugged areas of unmodified forest in the North Island. Some canoeists choose to continue downriver from Pipiriki. The lower reaches flow parallel to the Whanganui River Road for much of the way, through a mix of park and farmland and beside several Māori settlements.

Although several thousand people canoe the river every year, because of the one-way nature of travel it is usually possible to be paddling alone, or with just your group. There are three park huts (Whakahoro, John Coull and Tīeke Kāinga) along the river and 11 campsites (with water supply, toilets and cooking shelter) between Taumarunui and Pipiriki.

During the Great Walks season (1 October to 30 April) hut and campsite passes must be prepurchased. A hut warden is usually in residence at John Coull Hut during the season. Downes Hut, in the lower reaches near Ātene, is not part of the Great Walks system.

Tīeke Kāinga is located on one of many former Māori kāinga sites on the river and has been revived as a traditional marae, or village meeting ground. When Tīeke people are in residence, river travellers will be greeted by a traditional pōwhiri (welcome) that follows protocol,

A word of warning

This is a true story. Not so many years ago two young conservation staff arrived to work in Whanganui National Park. Their first task was to embark on a canoe trip to familiarise themselves with the river, and no doubt they set off thinking this was a pretty good job they'd landed. As most river travellers do, they stopped at the Mangapurua Landing, pulled their canoe onto the bank, and wandered along the 40-minute walking track to see the historic Bridge to Nowhere. The weather was fine, but when they returned to the landing they were greeted with the sight of their canoe floating away downriver – around a corner and out of sight. They realised the river had risen significantly during their walk, owing to rain falling somewhere else in its huge catchment.

And so they were stranded on the landing, 30 km by flooded river from the nearest road, with no transport, no cellphone coverage, and their warm clothes, tent and food floating downstream. Then, it started raining heavily.

The boys spent a long night squashed together in a small long-drop toilet, sharing a packet of biscuits they'd fortuitously taken on their walk. There was a happy ending – the next day a jetboat driver came to their rescue. He'd discovered their canoe several kilometres downriver, gear and food intact, and continued upriver to find the 'missing pieces'.

including the offer of a koha, or gift, by visitors to the marae. Visitors will be met first at the riverbank and these protocols will be explained. Food is usually cooked and shared together, in a communal way. When Tīeke people are not in residence, travellers are welcome to use the dining room, bunkroom and camping area.

From the river there are several short walks to historic features, such as the Hauhau niu poles at Maraekōwhai and the Bridge to Nowhere in the Mangapurua Valley. A river guidebook and brochures giving full details are available from the Department of Conservation. Several companies offer guided river trips, and canoes or kayaks can be hired from local outlets.

Jetboating

Jetboats have long been a popular form of transport and recreation on the Whanganui. Several commercial companies run tourist trips and provide charter transport services for trampers and hunters. Probably the most popular trips are from Pipiriki, heading upriver through some stunning river gorges and taking in the 40-minute walk from the Mangapurua Landing to the Bridge to Nowhere.

Though jetboats may seem a noisy intrusion to canoeists enjoying a wilderness experience on the river, they generally pass by quickly and cause only brief interruption. Department of Conservation staff undertake regular jetboat patrols during the Great Walks season, servicing facilities and providing assistance if needed.

Short walks

Te Maire (near Taumarunui) 2 hours loop
A gentle climb through a fine example of the podocarp forest that once covered much of the central North Island. There is a fine lookout point, plus a picinic area and swimming hole, along the way.

Ātene Viewpoint Walk (Whanganui River Road) 2 hours return

A walking track climbs gently through typical Whanganui forest of kāmahi, tawa, hīnau and pigeonwood trees as well as understorey shrubs, vines and ferns to a point overlooking an old cut-off meander. This is where the Whanganui River once flowed, around a long, narrow peninsula, before it cut a more direct passage. The walking track is at the northern end of the longer Ātene Skyline Track (see below).

Longer walk

Ātene Skyline Track (Whanganui River Road) 6 to 8 hours loop

A steady, steep climb following a forest-covered ridge around the back of a cut-off meander of the Whanganui River. This tramping track starts and finishes at river level and the highest point is Taumata Trig (523 m). There is one clearing at the track's halfway point, where there is drinking water, a shelter and toilet. At the northern end for some 3 km the track follows an old, gently graded roadline (built in 1959 during hydro power investigations), then joins with the Ātene Viewpoint Walk. Despite the forest cover there are several outlooks through the trees taking in the old meander, the river and its tributary valleys and, in the northern distance, Mt Ruapehu. The two track entrances are 2 km apart. Secure, private car parking is available (by donation) at Ātene.

Multi-day tramping trips

There are two major tramping opportunities in the park. Both require jetboat transport; this needs to be prearranged.

Mangapurua/Kaiwhakauka Track 3 to 4 days

The Mangapurua and Kaiwhakauka are two tributary valleys of the Whanganui that saddle with each other. Soldier-settlers' attempts to develop farms in these valleys following World War I lend a unique historic association to this track. At peak settlement time there were up to 30 farms in the Mangapurua and 16 in the Kaiwhakauka, with a road pushed through from Raetihi and a major concrete bridge constructed in the lower Mangapurua to provide access to riverboat transport. The settlers cleared the virgin forest and tried to transform it to farmland. However, problems such as poor access, erosion, regeneration, wild pig damage and falling stock prices during the 1930s Depression forced most of them to walk away.

Their legacy today is a unique tramping opportunity, a 40 km track that follows former roadlines through grassy clearings and regenerating native forest, past old homestead sites and, most dramatically, over the Mangapurua Bridge to Nowhere, possibly the sturdiest bridge ever built to be used only by walkers.

The only hut is at Whakahoro, at the track's northern end, but there is an abundance of great campsites on open grassy flats, some with toilets and all with plenty of side streams for water. Signs throughout the valleys identify homestead sites of the former settlers. The track's southern end meets the Whanganui River 30 km upriver from Pipiriki. Jetboat transport can be chartered to carry walkers to Pipiriki or back to their Whakahoro starting point.

Matemateaonga Track 3 to 4 days

In contrast to the modified Mangapurua/Kaiwhakauka Track, the Matemateaonga passes through the heart of the park's pristine forest. For much of its 42 km length the track follows the ridgeline of the Matemateaonga Range, and from vantage points along the way there are impressive views of rugged, dissected country that's clothed in a blanket of native forest as far as the eye can see. There are occasional glimpses of the mountains of Tongariro National Park to the east and, looking west, Mt Taranaki/Egmont.

Most of the track was originally formed as a road in the early 20th century, following ambitious plans to link Taranaki with Raetihi and the main trunk railway. Farming blocks were also surveyed, but the steep and rugged land held little potential for farming and the proposed through road did not eventuate.

Dense stands of tawa and kāmahi make up more than half the forest canopy along the track, while northern rātā and mixed podocarp species are scattered throughout. There is no beech forest. Native bird life is plentiful and includes less common species such as whiteheads.

There are three huts and one shelter, all with water supply. Camping space is limited on the narrow ridge track. The track starts at Kohi Saddle in Taranaki, 25 km east of Stratford, and ends at the Whanganui River, 21 km upriver from Pipiriki.

Whanganui River Road historic drive

For hundreds of years, Māori people living along the Whanganui used the river for access. Since the 1930s, however, villages on the lower reaches have been linked with the outside world by the Whanganui River Road. The road took 30 years to build, and the occurrence of floods and slips that caused construction delays then still hampers travel from time to time. Nevertheless, the road today provides access for several hundred people resident along the lower river.

For visitors it offers a fascinating scenic drive through several enclaves of the park. There are many heritage features, for example a restored 1850s flour mill, hand-cut tunnel culvert, historic park hut and the church at Jerusalem (Hiruhārama), where Home of Compassion founder Mother Aubert established a mission and orphanage in the late 19th century. There are several marae with traditional wharenui (meeting houses) at villages along the road. While travellers are welcome to admire these from a distance, visits onto the marae are by invitation only. Many villages have dual names, a result of the transliteration of biblical names bestowed by missionaries.

The Whanganui River Road starts 14 km from Wanganui city, off SH4. It climbs over the steep hill Aramoana (meaning 'path to the sea'), then winds alongside the river for 65 km, through the settlements of Parakino, Ātene (Athens), Koriniti (Corinth), Matahiwi, Rānana (London), Jerusalem (Hiruhārama) and, finally, Pipiriki. From there the road turns away from the river and continues for 28 km to Raetihi.

Top tips

■ Try a winter river trip. Winters in the valley are generally mild, there are fewer people on the river and, if it does rain, the waterfalls will be even more stunning.

■ If canoeing is not for you, a jetboat trip from Pipiriki to the Mangapurua Landing will give a glimpse of the river's best scenery and a gentle walk to the Bridge to Nowhere, a fascinating piece of New Zealand's heritage.

■ Seize three good photo opportunities on the Whanganui River Road: Whanganui River Valley (from the top of Aramoana Hill), the church (from the road just south of Jerusalem), and the river gorge and waterfall (from the viewpoint high above the river between Jerusalem and Pipiriki).

■ Easily accessible walking options are limited in the park. For a chance to stretch your legs and enjoy the bush without too much drama, explore the Ātene Viewpoint Walk. The gently graded track leads to an excellent lookout.

All villages, historic sites and other features of interest are described in the park brochure 'In and Around Whanganui National Park'. Pipiriki has a public shelter, toilets and riverside picnic area. Other accommodation options include farmstays, self-catering cottages, a private camping ground and a lodge. If self-driving, take your time, keep left on the many blind corners and make plenty of stops to enjoy the scenery and heritage sites. Alternatively, travel with a guided tour, which generally incorporates a marae visit.

Hunting

Recreational hunting of introduced pigs, fallow deer and goats is encouraged in the park. Boats are necessary for access to many hunting areas and commercial jetboat companies are available for charter. Hunting permits can be obtained from Department of Conservation offices. Note that from 1 October to 30 April hunting is not permitted in the Whanganui River valley within the park, and between 20 December and 20 February and during Easter hunting is not permitted within 200 m of tramping tracks.

Information

Getting there: There are daily air services from Auckland to Wanganui, as well as regular bus services from other main centres. From Wanganui the Whanganui River Road provides access to the southern end of the park and Pipiriki. There is also road access to Pipiriki from Raetihi (off SH4) and road access to Whakahoro, gateway to the central region of the park, from Ōwhango and Raurimu (also off SH4). In the north, Taumarunui is served by daily bus and rail services. In the west, there is road access to the Matemateaonga Track off the Stratford/Ōhura Road (SH43). River guiding companies have bases in various towns close to the park.

When to go: All activities can be undertaken and enjoyed at any time of the year, though most guided river trips operate during summer only.

Climate: Mild with few extremes, subject to moist, westerly airflows but also long periods of fine weather. Snow is rare.

Accommodation and facilities: A range of accommodation, shops, restaurants and services are available in Wanganui, Taumarunui and Ohakune (1 hour's drive from Pipiriki). There are a few accommodation options (lodges, homestays, self-catered) in the park and along the Whanganui River Road. In the park, there are several park huts and campsites for river travellers and trampers. There are also riverside campsites accessible by road at Ohinepane (21 km from Taumarunui), Whakahoro (44 km from Ōwhango and Raurimu on SH4) and Otumaire (Whanganui River Road, 40 km from Wanganui).

Commercial ventures: Guided canoeing trips, canoe/kayak hire, cultural tours, jetboat charters, Whanganui River Road tours.

Further reading: Whanganui Parkmap; NZMS 260 series topographical maps R19, R20, S20, S21; park brochures; *Guide to the Whanganui River*, New Zealand Canoeing Association; *Historical Map of the Mangapurua Valley*, Four Friends Trust.

Special conditions: The Whanganui River can rise by several metres in a short space of time. Even if is not raining where you are, rainfall elsewhere in the river's huge catchment can quickly affect the Whanganui's flow. When stopping, pull your canoe high up the bank and tie it to something secure. If the river is in heavy flood, don't try to canoe – if you capsize you might get swept downriver and be unable to get back in your craft or to the river's edge.

Canoeists and jetboaters on the river need to show consideration for each other. The protocol is that canoeists head to the right when facing jetboats coming upriver, and stop to let jetboats headed downriver to overtake. Turn your canoe at right angles to the wake. Remember that jetboats cannot stop or slow down in rapids.

Visitor centres: There is a Department of Conservation office in Wanganui where information is available about the river journey, tramping tracks, road access and licensed tour operators. Brochures, maps, hut and campsite tickets and hunting permits can be obtained. The Department of Conservation field centres in Pipiriki and Taumarunui are not always staffed. The Wanganui i-SITE and visitor information centres in Ohakune, Stratford and Taumarunui can also provide information on tourism operations in the park.

DOC Wanganui
Cnr St Hill and Ingestre Streets
Wanganui
Phone 0-6-348 8475
Email wanganuiconservancy@doc.govt.nz
Open Monday to Friday 8 am to 5 pm; closed on public holidays

Nelson Lakes National Park

Location: northern end of the Southern Alps/Kā Tiritiri o te Moana, South Island

Features: lakes ■ mountains ■ forests ■ long, open valleys and tussocklands ■ Rotoiti Nature Recovery Project

Activities: short walks ■ tramping ■ boating ■ ski-touring ■ climbing ■ birdwatching ■ hunting ■ fishing

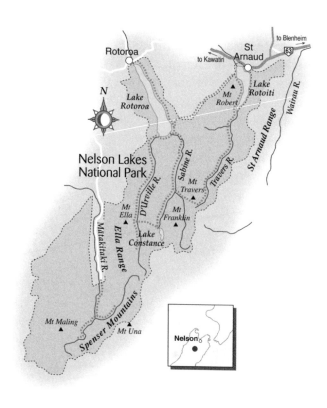

The landscape combination of mountains, beech forests, lakes and wide-open river valleys that is so typical of South Island national parks is particularly well represented in Nelson Lakes.

The park is named for its two lakes, Rotoiti and Rotoroa (meaning 'small lake' and 'long lake' respectively), which nestle in picturesque grandeur between steep, forested and often snow-covered mountain ranges. The two lakes are among the largest in New Zealand with largely unmodified catchments. The park's mountains extend far to the south, beyond the lakes, in a 75 km-long expanse of ranges that make up the northern end of the Southern Alps/Kā Tiritiri o te Moana.

There is a great range of recreation opportunities in the park. Tramping, climbing, ski-touring, boating, fishing and wandering short forest walks, in particular engaging with the prolific bird life at Rotoiti, are the most popular activities in the park.

About the park

While the park's mountains have been thrust upwards by tectonic forces along the South Island's Alpine Fault, lakes Rotoiti and Rotoroa are the most obvious legacies of the mighty force of ice. During successive ice ages, some time between 10,000 and 20,000 years ago, the lakebeds were gouged by glaciers, then filled with water as the ice retreated. The Travers, Sabine, D'Urville and Mātakitaki Valleys are classic U-shaped, glacier-gouged formations, lined by mountain ranges with arête peaks, cirques and alpine meadows where tarns and wetlands have formed in depressions left as the great glaciers retreated.

These ice-sculptured landscapes are enhanced today by vast beech forests that clothe the mountainsides and valley floors. Four of New Zealand's beech species grow in the park, in forests also filled with the rich and varied greens of sub-canopy trees and shrubs and ferns, mosses and lichens that can seem almost fairy-like in the ever-changing light so characteristic of beech forests.

The park's forests support some of New Zealand's more significant and threatened species, such as long-tailed bats and land snails. Visitors are more likely to see the big, playful and colourful bush parrots called South Island kākā, smaller kākāriki, New Zealand's only endemic raptor the New Zealand falcon, and friendly, ground-hopping South Island robin. The prolific presence of honey-eating tūī and bellbirds can be vouched for daily by tuning into their usually rousing 'dawn chorus'.

Above about 900 m the beech forests become stunted, then give way to a wonderful diversity of natural ecosystems, including tussockfields, rock and scree slopes, tarns, wetlands and meadows filled with alpine flowers, herbs and grasses. These mountaintops are the domain of ground-hopping pipits, thousands of alpine grasshoppers, the occasional tiny rock wren and the kākā's cheeky alpine relation, the kea. In summer (on a good day) these are wonderful places for trampers to wander; in winter they are often covered with snow and ice and in such conditions should be left to those with climbing experience and equipment.

Legendary importance

The lakes of the park are of special significance to local Māori. According to legend, Rotoiti and Rotoroa were the first of all the great lakes throughout the South Island to have been created by an ancestral chief named Ra kai hau tu, who used his kō (digging stick) to dig massive hollows in the ground as he travelled southwards through the island.

Ra kai hau tu filled these holes with water and food (fish and waterfowl), which later became an important food source for Māori as they passed by on their way to the greenstone sources of the West Coast.

While the lakes and valleys of Nelson Lakes provided routes for early Māori travellers and European explorers, apart from a brief period of farming in some of the lower valleys this previously remote, mountainous region has been left largely undisturbed by humans. Protection of natural values has been assured since the national park was created in 1956. The popularity of the park as a holiday and outdoor recreation playground has steadily increased.

Although it flows outside the park, mention should be made of the mighty Buller (Kawatiri) River. The Buller is sourced from nearly all of the park's lakes and rivers, and with so much of its catchment protected it is the largest substantially unmodified river in New Zealand. Its wild and scenic character makes it popular for rafting, kayaking and fishing.

What to do

Short walks

Bellbird Track (St Arnaud) 15 minutes loop
A glimpse into the lakeside honeydew beech forests of the Rotoiti Nature Recovery Project. You won't have to walk far to be greeted by the resident bird population – songs of the nectar-feeding tūī and bellbirds will be resounding from the forest, big colourful kākā might greet you, little South Island robins will be watching from the forest floor and fantails and tomtits will be darting about, searching for insects. Take time to read the excellent information panels, which describe the success story of the recovery project. The path is suitable for wheelchairs.

Honeydew Walk (St Arnaud) 45 minutes return
A longer look at the Rotoiti Nature Recovery Project that starts on the Bellbird Track (above). This walk continues further into the red and mountain beech trees, with their trunks and branches blackened by the honeydew-producing insects the nectar-eating birds, insects and lizards rely on for food. More signs tell the story of this beech forest and the recovery it has made since conservation staff declared war on pests such as wasps, rodents, possums and stoats. If you have only time or fitness for one undemanding walk in the park, this is the one to choose.

Rotoiti Nature Recovery Project

One of the success stories of New Zealand conservation has taken place in a pocket of beech forest beside Lake Rotoiti. The Rotoiti Nature Recovery Project was created in 1997 to enhance and protect around 800 ha. It was expanded in 2001 and it today extends to 5000 ha.

The project is one of the country's first 'mainland island' projects, where concentrated efforts to control animal pests have resulted in forest and native wildlife recovery. Surrounding communities, through the volunteer group Friends of Rotoiti, have thrown their weight behind the Department of Conservation's goal to restore the region's honeydew beech forests by extending the area of control of wasps, possums, rodents and stoats.

The sweet honeydew that gives these forests their character is produced by sap-sucking insects living in the beech tree trunks. This should provide food for native birds, insects and lizards, but it became monopolised by introduced wasps. The Rotoiti project quickly made an impact: within two years wasp numbers were seasonally reduced by 90 per cent and possum numbers cut to nearly zero. Early results included record breeding seasons of kā kā and increased numbers of South Island robins. In 2004 several great spotted kiwi, roroa, were reintroduced to the project area, having not been seen or heard in the park since the 1920s. The new arrivals came from one of the species' last strongholds, Kahurangi National Park, and settled happily in their new home.

One of the reasons for selecting Rotoiti as a 'mainland island' was its easy access. Already more than 90,000 annual visitors are attracted to this very scenic part of the park. New tracks, including one suitable for wheelchairs, comprehensive information displays and the chance to hear a restored dawn chorus and evening kiwi calls, and enjoy the playful antics of a growing kākā population, will surely entice yet more.

Brunner Peninsula Nature Walk (St Arnaud) 1.5 hours loop

A pleasant, scenic walk around the peninsula at the end of Lake Rotoiti, between Kerr Bay and West Bay, which happens to cross the main South Island Alpine Fault. A longer option (add an hour) is to return via Rotoiti Lodge and Ward Street, which leads through a variety of native vegetation and has several good access points to the lakeshore.

Rotoroa Nature Walk (Rotoroa) 25 minutes loop

A pretty walk showing the greatest diversity of all the short walks in the park. It follows the lakeshore then loops back through beech and podocarp trees, with shrubs, vines and ferns growing beneath.

Braeburn Walk (Rotoroa) 1.5 hours loop

An easy wander for most of the way, first following a delightful avenue of tree fuchsias. This gnarled and twisted, red papery-barked tree is the world's largest fuchsia and one of New Zealand's few native deciduous trees. Known to Māori as kōtukutuku, its flowers change in colour from green to an attractive deep burgundy. Other forest here is a profusion of mature beech and podocarp trees, rich in bird life. Curious robins might follow you as you climb briefly at the end of the track to view the pretty Braeburn Falls tumbling down a shaded, mossy bank.

Longer walks

Lake Rotoiti Circuit (St Arnaud) 7 to 9 hours loop

The walking time can be more than halved by taking a water taxi part of the way. Lakehead Track follows the eastern Rotoiti shore from St Arnaud to Lakehead Hut. The walk leads through beech forest, with northern rātā trees flowering red in summer and a rare (for this park) stand of rimu trees along the way. Tūī, bellbirds, fantails, robins and kākā will likely accompany you. If the Travers River is low, you can cross at the lakehead, otherwise there is a swingbridge 1.5 hours further up the Travers Valley.

Lakeside Track follows the western lakeshore, starting from Mt Robert Road. A feature about 2.5 hours along the shore is Whisky Falls, which tumble 40 m in this glacier-shaped hanging valley. An illicit whisky still found here in the 1880s gives the falls their name.

Water taxis can be chartered to meet you at the lakehead. Coldwater Hut Jetty and Lakehead Jetty are the two water taxi drop-off points.

Mt Robert (St Arnaud) 5 hours loop

Pick a good day so you can enjoy the stunning views. There are two tracks that climb onto the broad, open, northern face of Mt Robert, which overlooks Lake Rotoiti and St Arnaud. Both tracks start within 500 m of each other on the Mt Robert road. Pinchgut Track begins in the forest, then soon emerges onto the open face of Mt Robert. Zigzagging up this face, the track alternates between open and forested areas, breaking out into alpine tussock tops at the crest of the hill adjacent to the Bush Edge Shelter. The track continues on a gentle gradient from here, becoming the Robert Ridge Route just beyond the Relax Shelter. Paddy's Track cuts across scree-filled gullies then climbs to Bushline Hut and crosses the open, tussock-covered northern face to meet with Pinchgut Track.

Much of the forest cover on Mt Robert was cleared and burnt by settler farmers from the 1880s. Erosion scarps remain, and the fragile plant life will take years to recover in the exposed terrain. Nevertheless, there are alpine shrublands, red tussocklands and herbfields to explore, and the views are great.

There are two shelters and one hut on this circuit. Carry water, and be prepared for changeable weather. Mt Robert is covered with snow at times in winter.

Multi-day tramping trips

The park's long river valleys are linked by alpine passes, providing great natural routes that, in good summertime weather, are negotiable by most trampers. There are many tramping options; following are those that are most popular and best serviced with park facilities.

Lake Angelus (St Arnaud) 2 days

One of the park's most popular overnight trips explores a stunning alpine landscape. The hut perches high on the mountains between Rotoroa and Rotoiti, in a basin beside the small Lake Angelus. In good weather it is a great base for botanising in the surrounding herbfields, bogs and tussock slopes, or for short walks to great lookout points.

The most direct approach is along Robert Ridge, which is broad at first, narrowing and becoming rocky further south. The views are stunning in good weather but offer neither shelter nor escape routes should the weather deteriorate – as it often does. This route begins as the Pinchgut Track at the Mt Robert car park, 5 km from St Arnaud.

Also starting from here is the Speargrass Track. This leads through beech forest to Speargrass Hut, then follows a poled route up Speargrass Creek to join Robert Ridge just before Lake Angelus.

Cascade Track is the most varied approach. It branches off the Travers Track about an hour from the head of Lake Rotoiti then climbs up Hūkere Stream, through forest then above the bushline and ends with a steep pitch between bluffs and waterfalls. This section of the track can become impassable after heavy rain.

It is easy to underestimate the difficulty of a Lake Angelus trip. All three routes are highly exposed in sections, prone to changeable and adverse weather conditions at any time of year and marked only with occasional poles above the bushline. There can also be a risk of avalanches, especially after snowstorms. If the weather deteriorates for your trip out, the most sheltered route is via Speargrass Creek, even though it starts with an icy climb out of the Angelus basin. In winter the lake is frozen and snow covers the higher sections of all routes.

Although Lake Angelus Hut has been extended to cope with demand, it operates on a first-come, first-served basis and is regularly full.

Travers–Sabine Circuit (St Arnaud) 4 to 7 days

A classic New Zealand tramping trip that starts from Lake Rotoiti, follows the Travers Valley to its head, crosses an alpine saddle then descends the Sabine Valley to Lake Rotoroa and returns to Rotoiti through low-level beech forest. The main features are grassy river flats, beech forests, wetlands, waterfalls, mountain lakes and the ever-present 2000 m mountain ranges looming along both valleys. There's a chance, too, of being visited by a curious kea on the mountaintops.

Most of the 80 km circuit is a well-marked tramping track and most rivers and streams are bridged. The exception is the alpine crossing over Travers Saddle, which is an unformed but poled route. The saddle is high above the bushline and can be subject to poor visibility, high winds and freezing temperatures at any time of the year.

There are seven huts on the circuit and camping is permitted, though fires aren't. Side trips worth considering are Lake Angelus (3 to 4 hours up Cascade Track), Cupola Basin Hut (2.5 hours' steep climb) and Blue Lake (3.5 hours to a delightful alpine lake).

Mātakitaki and Glenroy Valleys

More remote tramping experiences in less-visited regions can be found in the Mātakitaki and Glenroy Valleys to the west of the park.

Alpine passes

Challenging trips for those with suitable experience and equipment cross alpine passes in the mountainous heart of the park. Most popular is a multi-day expedition from Blue Lake Hut in the upper Sabine Valley, over Waiau Pass to the St James Walk. A second option is from Blue Lake Hut over Moss Pass to the park's D'Urville Valley, an avalanche-prone route. Closer, and shorter, is the crossing from the Travers Valley to either Sabine or Lake Angelus Huts via Hopeless Creek and Sunset Saddle.

Mountaineering

Although not so alluring as the major peaks of the more southern national parks, the many 2000 m peaks in Nelson Lakes present a range of challenging climbing routes. The scale is perhaps not so great as the big southern peaks, but the moderate weather and smaller scale of the

Top tips

- Tune in to the dawn chorus on the Bellbird or Honeydew Track. It's one of the best you'll hear. In the evenings, listen for the distinctive screeches of the recently reintroduced great spotted kiwi, roroa, on the eastern side of Lake Rotoiti.
- Take a water taxi to the head of Lake Rotoiti and wander back around the lakeshore.
- The Travers–Sabine Circuit is one of New Zealand's finest back-country walks outside of the Great Walks. The best direction to walk is up the Travers and down the Sabine – Travers Saddle is easier to cross this way.
- Walk, boat or take a water taxi to the head of Lake Rotoroa and base yourself at Sabine or D'Urville Hut for some tramping, fishing and hunting recreation.
- Visit the Nelson Lakes National Park Visitor Centre. There's an excellent audiovisual presentation and range of displays about the park's natural and human history. Good for a rainy day.
- See stunning alpine scenery on a 2 or 3 day tramping trip up the Sabine Valley to Blue Lake Hut.

Nelson Lakes peaks lend appeal for summer climbs, with the tramp in being as much a feature as the climb. Winter climbs nevertheless provide ample challenge, such as routes on the south face of Mt Hopeless, the south-west ridge of Mt Travers. Some of the best climbs are along the Spenser Mountains at the very southern end of the park, notably Mt Una, Faerie Queene, Enid and Humboldt.

Ski-touring

In good snow years there are excellent ski-touring opportunities along the Robert Ridge.

Boating

Recreational boating and sailing are traditional pastimes in the park, and jetties and ramps are provided on both Rotoiti and Rotoroa. Waterskiing is not permitted. Powered craft are not permitted on the rivers of the park. Scenic cruises are available from local operators. Kayaking is also a popular and obviously more peaceful means of exploring the forest-lined bays and beaches of both lakes. Rowboats and kayaks can be hired and guided kayak trips are available on Rotoiti.

Fishing

Introduced brown trout are present in the park's lakes and rivers and lake trolling or river fly-fishing are popular. Fishing guides are available at St Arnaud, Rotoroa and Murchison. Fishing licences are required.

Hunting

Recreational hunting of introduced red deer and chamois is encouraged. Permits are available from the park visitor centre of any Department of Conservation office in the Nelson/Marlborough region.

Mountain biking

Although mountain biking is not permitted in the park there are excellent rides close by. The Rainbow Road (112 km to Hanmer Springs) follows an old stock route just east of the park. Permission is required and details are available at the park visitor centre. There are also mountain-biking options to Beebys Knob, a steep 700 m climb in neighbouring Mt Richmond Forest Park, and shorter, easier rides on Porika and Braeburn Roads, near the park. Specific mountain-bike trails are marked through the Teetotal Recreation Area only a few kilometres from St Arnaud.

Rafting

Just outside the park, the Buller River, with its granite canyons and big volumes of clean mountain water, is one of New Zealand's premier rafting rivers. Rafting companies in Murchison offer both whitewater excitement and more gentle family and beginner trips.

Information

Getting there: The main gateway to the park is St Arnaud, a small township on SH63, 1.5 hours' drive from both Blenheim and Nelson. The second main entrance is at Rotoroa, 40 km west of St Arnaud. An 11 km road leads from SH6 up Gowan Valley Road to Rotoroa. Daily bus services are available to St Arnaud, though some of these services are reduced to three times a week over the winter months.

When to go: Summer for tramping, winter for climbing and ski-touring. Year-round for short walks, photography and nature appreciation.

Climate: Relatively mild temperatures but prone to year-round rainfall. Snow in winter. Above the bushline, snow and storms can occur suddenly at any time of the year.

Accommodation and facilities: Accommodation at St Arnaud includes hostels, rental baches (small holiday homes), motels, tourist lodges and two park camping areas, each with showers, toilets, laundry, powered sites, tent sites and picnic areas for day visitors. There is also a restaurant, café, shop, postal facilities and petrol at St Arnaud. Rotoroa has a self-register park camping area, bed-and-breakfast and lodge accommodation, but no other facilities. Murchison, less than 1 hour's drive from St Arnaud, has campgrounds, motels, hotels, cafés, restaurants and shops. Blenheim and Nelson are cities with all services. There are more than 20 huts throughout the park.

Commercial ventures: Water taxis operate on demand on Rotoiti and Rotoroa and tramper shuttle services run seasonally to all major park entrances, also on demand. Scenic cruises are available on the lakes and fishing guides operate from St Arnaud, Rotoroa and Murchison. Kayaks and rowboats are available for hire on Rotoiti.

Further reading: Nelson Lakes Parkmap; NZMS 260 series topographical maps N29, M29, M30, M31; *Climbing Guide to the Nelson Lakes Region*, Simon Noble, revised by Ben Winnubst.

Special conditions: Wasps can be a nuisance in the park, especially in late summer and autumn (February to April). Carry suitable medication if allergic to stings. Insect repellent for sandflies is also advisable.

Animal pest control using toxins and traps is regularly undertaken in the Rotoiti Nature Recovery Project area, on the north-east side of Lake Rotoiti. If visiting this area, keep to the marked tracks and do not tamper with bait stations or traps.

Remember that much of the park is in an alpine environment. Bad weather can occur at any time of the year and much of the park is snow-covered in winter. Travel through snow should only be attempted by those with suitable experience and equipment. Be wary of avalanches. Not all streams are bridged and they can be impassable after heavy rain.

Visitor centre: The park visitor centre at St Arnaud offers information and advice, maps, brochures, hut tickets, hunting permits and fishing licences. There is also an excellent audiovisual presentation about the Buller River as well as informative displays about the park.

Nelson Lakes National Park Visitor Centre
View Road
PO Box 55
St Arnaud
Phone 0-3-521 1806
Email starnaudAO@doc.govt.nz
Open daily 8.30 am to 4.30 pm (hours extended in summer)

Abel Tasman National Park

Location: northern coast of the South Island

Features: sweeping golden beaches ▪ lagoons ▪ estuaries ▪ sculptured granite headlands ▪ inland forests and limestone karst landscapes

Activities: short walks ▪ tramping ▪ sea kayaking ▪ swimming ▪ snorkelling ▪ marine mammal watching

Abel Tasman is the smallest of New Zealand's parks and, because of its stunning coastline, one of the most popular. Golden beaches, estuaries and lagoons are lined by young regenerating forest. Diverse habitats in the park support a range of bush birds, sea birds and wetland species. A marine reserve adjoining part of the park protects the marine environment, and fur seals, dolphins and sometimes whales frequent the sheltered waters offshore. Inland, on the park's lesser-known high country, are steep hills covered with beech forest and the almost surreal marble karst landscape of Canaan Downs.

Each year thousands of trampers follow the gentle forest tracks, cross the estuaries and wander the beaches of the Abel Tasman Coast Track, New Zealand's most popular Great Walk. Sea kayakers, sometimes accompanied by seals and dolphins, paddle into inlets and lagoons and through the waters of Tonga Island Marine Reserve, and camp in remote bays accessible only by sea. Many more people explore these features on day trips – the park's coastline is easy to reach by private or commercial boats. A network of short walks explores coastal formations, historic Māori sites and karst limestone features.

The park is a favourite summer holiday spot for New Zealanders and is increasingly being discovered by international visitors, to the extent that park management is encouraging people to visit during winter to spread the numbers. Winters are generally mild and settled. The scenery is still stunning.

About the park

Abel Tasman is arguably the most modified of all New Zealand's national parks. For several hundred years Māori people lived along the coast in seasonal fishing and gardening villages. From the mid 19th century European settlers logged forests, quarried granite and burnt the hillsides to create pasture. Farming, never a viable option on the harsh granite soils, was short-lived. During the early 20th century people from the Nelson region, attracted by the charms of the coastline, established holiday homes in the bays and inlets. Their concern over logging operations, spearheaded by local conservationist Perrine Moncrieff, inspired a successful campaign to create a national park.

The park was named after Dutch explorer Abel Tasman, the first European to visit New Zealand, though his short stay was marred by a fatal skirmish with Māori people along this coastline that resulted in the death of four of his crew. The park was established in 1942, 300 years after Tasman's brief visit.

Today regenerating mānuka and kānuka forests, mixed with some black beech, cover the coastal hills. In the more fertile, damp gullies, where regeneration is faster, a richer variety of broad-leafed shrubs, tree ferns, vines and kiekie thrives. Tūī, bellbirds, fantails and kererū are the main forest birds in the park; riflemen, South Island kākā, kea and kākāriki are also present.

It is the coastline of the park that is best known. Granite forms the bedrock, and weathering and wave action against this hard rock have sculptured diverse and distinctive coastal landforms: islands,

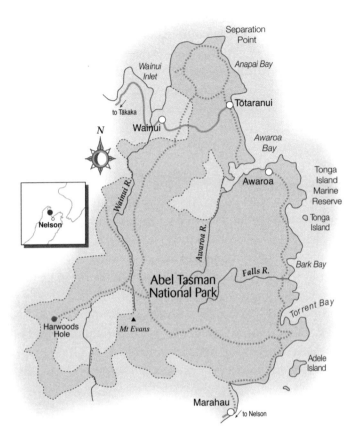

reefs, rock stacks, wave-cut platforms, rounded boulders and rocky headlands.

The park's famous golden beaches are made up of sparkling weathered particles of quartz, mica and golden feldspars, minerals eroded from granite and carried to the sea by streams, then swept along the coast by currents and tides. The 4 m tidal range here is one of the highest in the country. The park's characteristic crescent bays were eroded from basins of less resistant rock between ridges of harder rocks. The result is an intricate variety of sandspits and bars, such as those at Torrent Bay and Bark Bay, shallow estuaries like Awaroa, and a golden procession of crescent beaches, for example Tōtaranui, Onetahuti Bay and Anchorage.

No other place in New Zealand contains the diversity of plant and animal communities as the park's sheltered coast. Barnacles, periwinkles, tube worms and seaweeds occupy tidal bands, underwater seaweeds are grazed by sea urchins and cat's eyes, while underwater reefs support coral-like beds of bryozoans, which are important habitats for fish. Above the waterline, the coastline provides habitat for large numbers of fur seals and is a breeding ground for little blue penguins.

Estuaries contain saltmarsh vegetation, rushes, glasswort and sea primroses. These sandy places are home to many fish, snails, worms and crabs, which are food for wading birds such as oystercatchers, pied stilts, white-faced herons, banded rails and reef herons. Weka and fernbirds also sometimes frequent wetland areas. Sea birds, such as Caspian and white-fronted terns, gulls, shags, fluttering shearwaters and Australasian gannets, dive offshore for fish.

The park's rivers and streams, which are mostly tea-coloured from tannins leached from the soil, are an important habitat for galaxiids and other native freshwater fish. Introduced trout, which prey on and compete with these native fish, prefer clear water and are rarely seen in the park's waterways.

Inland uplands

While much of the focus of Abel Tasman National Park is on the coast, the inland high country also contains significant natural features and landforms.

Canaan Downs sits at the northern end of a thick belt of ancient marble rock that extends through neighbouring Kahurangi National Park. The associated karst landscape, created by the dissolving action of water on the rock, contains strange and striking landforms – fluted rock, sinkholes, caves, vanishing streams and a complex subterranean drainage system.

A park road winds to the heart of Canaan Downs and a short track leads through beech forest to the rather eerie entrance to the Harwoods Hole sinkhole. It is impossible to see far into this chasm and a long way to fall, though cavers relish abseiling into its dark depths.

The park's uplands are blanketed by a mix of red, silver and mountain beech forest, regenerating trees and shrubs, ferns and bracken. The exception is Moa Park, a small enclave of red tussock, alpine herbs and flowers, which is the only subalpine area in the park.

What to do

Short walks

Abel Tasman Memorial (Golden Bay) 10 minutes return
A memorial and interpretive display here commemorate Dutch explorer Abel Tasman's visit in 1642. Tasman was the first European to discover New Zealand. Signposted on the western approach road to the park, this walk is outside the park boundary but a significant spot nevertheless, with a fine outlook across Golden Bay.

Wainui Falls (Golden Bay) 1.25 hours return
On the eastern side of the park, a gentle wander through tree ferns and mature northern rātā forest to these picturesque falls.

Headlands Track and Pukatea Walk (Tōtaranui) 1 hour loop
A shady hillside overlooking the Tōtaranui estuary with some mature beech forest, buttressed pukatea trees and massive northern rātā trees that were left untouched by farming settlers. A worthy detour en route is the smaller Pukatea Walk. The boardwalk approach through raupo swamp adds to the variety, and the viewpoint that takes in the sweeping golden sands of Tōtaranui and adjacent beaches, all the way to the

Awaroa estuary, is worth a prolonged rest. At low tide this walk can be approached across the Tōtaranui estuary.

Anapai Bay (Tōtaranui) 2 hours return

Part of the Abel Tasman Coast Track but a charming walk in its own right. Anapai is regarded as one of the park's most gorgeous bays, with rocky outcrops dividing the forest-framed beach, and fur seals likely to be cavorting in the shallows. The track climbs from Tōtaranui through dry kānuka forest then descends gently into a sheltered valley filled with more lush vegetation and on to Anapai Bay.

Goat Bay and Waiharakeke (Tōtaranui) 1.5 to 2 hours return

Heading south from Tōtaranui and a slightly easier climb over to Goat Bay (yet another gorgeous beach, this one lined with northern rātā forest), then a short forest walk to Waiharakeke Beach, which backs into swampland filled with regenerating kahikatea and pukatea species. This is also part of the Abel Tasman Coast Track but, if visiting Tōtaranui, it's a lovely short walk. The view from the headland between Tōtaranui and Goat Bay is a fine photo point.

Gibbs Hill (Tōtaranui) 2 to 3 hours return

A steep climb behind Tōtaranui Beach on a firebreak track, through mānuka regeneration and some weed patches. The track itself is not pretty, and it's a hot climb on a summer's day, but the views from the top ridgeline are superb, sweeping all the way from Farewell Spit and Golden Bay, past the mountains of Kahurangi National Park, to Nelson and round to D'Urville Island at the head of the Marlborough Sounds. This track also links with other park tracks.

Harwoods Hole (Canaan car park, off Tākaka Hill) 1.5 hours return

The park's peculiar karst limestone landscape has created the 176 m sinkhole known as Harwoods Hole, the deepest vertical shaft in New Zealand. A track leads through beech forest to a junction, the right-hand branch leading away from the hole to a lookout with spectacular views across fluted marble outcrops to the hinterland of the park. The left-hand branch provides access for cavers who sometimes explore the shaft itself. It is very dangerous to approach beyond the warning signs.

Moa Park (Canaan car park, off Tākaka Hill) 3.5 hours return

Part of the park's Inland Track, this climbs over two forest-covered saddles to the distinctive Moa Park clearing, with its subalpine tussocks and herbfields, surrounded by montane forest. Moa Park has occurred in a natural depression that has created a cool microclimate and boggy soils, hence the unusual plant associations growing at an altitude normally dominated by trees. Two short tracks beyond Moa Park lead to excellent viewpoints.

Multi-day tramping trips

There are two major tramping options in the park. Both require prearranged transport at one end, unless walked in a particularly long circuit. Several companies operate bus, water taxi and tramper shuttle services.

Abel Tasman Coast Track 3 to 5 days

One of New Zealand's most popular tramping tracks, and accordingly huts and campsites must be booked – check the Department of Conservation website for specific details. There are four huts and 19 campsites accessible to walkers along the coast, and track walkers are entitled to stay overnight at the major Tōtaranui campground. There is also some private lodge accommodation.

The superb coastline is this track's major drawcard. As the saying goes, life is a beach. On the Abel Tasman, significant sections of the 51 km track is in fact on beaches. When the route is not meandering along the golden sands, it winds gently over headlands or across vast tidal estuaries where wading birds fossick for food.

The track is of very high quality. All streams are bridged and the only consideration is to monitor tide times, as there are several estuary crossings that are possible only at low tide. Most people walk the section between Marahau and Tōtaranui, usually because of ease of access, but the section north of Tōtaranui is equally impressive.

Bus services link with Marahau, Tōtaranui and Wainui. Regular water taxis operate to beaches along the track. These also offer a pack-carrying service.

Inland Track 3 to 5 days

This lesser-known track penetrates the forested uplands of the park. It is rougher and steeper than the coast track, but rewards trampers with a mix of regenerating and mature forests and, from occasional granite outcrops, excellent lookout points. A feature of this walk is Moa Park, a small enclave of red tussock, alpine herbs and flowers, which is the only subalpine area in the park. The southern end of the 37.5 km track starts at Tinline Bay, on the coast near Marahau and the northern end starts (or finishes) at Wainui Bay. The track can be walked in sections, as there are also access points from Canaan Downs, off Tākaka Hill, via the Wainui River in the west of the park and from Pigeon Saddle, on the Tōtaranui Road. There are three huts (including Wainui Hut, which is just off the main track) and two shelters.

Sea kayaking

Abel Tasman is one national park where, in summer in particular, sea kayakers are almost as common as walkers. The park's coastline, its beaches, bays, inlets, estuaries, rocky headlands and little islets, is simply made for kayak exploration, and kayakers are able to gain a perspective not available to land-based travellers. In the Tonga Island Marine Reserve, for example, Mosquito Bay and Shag Harbour are tiny, remote coves only accessible by water.

Wildlife watching is an added bonus. Paddling through the water alongside fishing shags or gannets, quietly approaching sleeping fur seals on rocky outcrops, gliding beside a school of flatfish in a clear tidal estuary, or perhaps being accompanied across a sheltered bay by a little

Tonga Island Marine Reserve

Abel Tasman National Park is famous for its beaches, bays, estuaries and rocky headlands – areas that provide habitats for native birds, fish and other species. While national park status gives legal protection to the land, the creation of Tonga Island Marine Reserve has marked a new era in the protection of this special environment.

Since 1993 all marine life within the reserve has been protected. This means no fishing, no shellfish gathering, no polluting and no disturbance of marine life is allowed, though people are welcome to swim, dive, photograph and generally enjoy the increased marine life.

Tonga Island Marine Reserve has an area of nearly 2000 ha, stretching along 12 km of coastline. Many of the features of the park's granite coast are found within this area: sandy beaches, bouldery headlands and reefs, small estuaries and a sand-mud sea floor. The estuaries in particular link the marine reserve to the national park, creating a two-way buffer of protection.

The reserve benefits not only fish and shellfish, but also animals like seals, penguins, shags, herons, gannets and other sea birds. Native plants becoming rare on the mainland, such as the large-leafed whau and taupata, a *Coprosma* species, are protected on small islands within the reserve.

Now that fishing has stopped, populations of inshore fish such as wrasses, blue cod, snapper, tarakihi and moki are expected to increase. Crayfish in particular have already noticeably increased in size and number. As fish life in the reserve recovers, it is likely to improve fishing prospects outside its boundary.

New Zealand's first marine reserve was created in 1975. The number has since grown to 20, with several more proposals currently under investigation.

blue penguin or a pod of dolphins are all likely kayaking experiences along the Abel Tasman coast.

Several companies offer guided kayak trips, ranging from a few hours to overnight and multi-day options. Kayaks can also be hired, often with a package that includes basic instruction. Park huts and campsites are available for kayakers. As with walkers these must be booked. There are two campsites, Mosquito Bay and Observation Bay, that are only accessible by boat. The coastline between Marahau and the Awaroa headland is more sheltered. Beyond Awaroa the bay is prone to high winds and tidal currents.

Diving and snorkelling

The best way to explore the Tonga Island Marine Reserve, which adjoins the park, is to get into the water. Sea temperatures are not known for being particularly tepid here, but the water is clear. From land the best snorkelling is around the rocks to the south of the reserve, between Tonga Quarry and Foul Point. Scuba diving is more rewarding on reef systems at the northern end, at around 15 m depth.

There is a marked absence of seaweeds and a good likelihood of spotting any of the abundance of grazing animals present, such as kina (sea eggs) and turban shells. An attractive pink algae covers much of the underwater rock, while caves and crevices are likely to be hiding crayfish or conger eels. Fish species most likely to be spotted include wrasses, blue cod, snapper, tarakihi and moki.

Caving

Harwoods Hole drops 176 m down a vertical shaft to an underground river that emerges from the ground and flows into Gorge Creek and eventually the Tākaka River. Abseiling into the hole then following the underground river to its emergence is sometimes attempted by experienced cavers. Note this is *not* an activity for novices. It is a regular

Above: Waiau Pass, an alpine crossing in the heart of Nelson Lakes National Park. The pass is snow-covered in winter. (DP) Below: The glacier-formed Blue Lake, a popular tramping destination in the Upper Sabine Valley, Nelson Lakes National Park. (SB)

Opposite top: Crossing Travers River in Nelson Lakes National Park. Long, mountain-lined valleys, such as the Travers and Sabine, provide excellent tramping routes in the park. (SB)

Opposite bottom: Rotoiti, one of the two major, glacier-gouged mountain-surrounded lakes of Nelson Lakes National Park. (SB)

Right: Ground-hopping South Island robins are likely to make themselves known to visitors in South Island national parks. (SB)

Below: Distinctive karst limestone rock formations in beech forest near Harwoods Hole, Abel Tasman National Park uplands. (DP)

Above: The sheltered, forest-fringed coastline of Abel Tasman National Park is ideal for sea kayakers. (DP)

Left: Pied shag, one of several shag species that thrive in the estuarine and coastal habitats of Abel Tasman National Park. (SB)

Opposite top: Te Pukatea Bay. Golden sand beaches are a stunning feature of Abel Tasman National Park. (SB)

Opposite bottom: Family park – Abel Tasman Coast Track is suitable for all ages and abilities. Much of the track follows the beach. (SB)

Opposite: Tidal flats at Marahau, entrance point to Abel Tasman National Park. (SB)

Right: On the Lockett Range. Kahurangi, New Zealand's second-largest national park, offers a huge range of tramping opportunities. (DP)

Below left: Limestone formations provide natural shelters in Kahurangi, such as Upper Gridiron Shelter on the Flora Track. (SB)

Below right: Gentian, Mt Owen, Kahurangi National Park. (SB)

Adelaide Tarn, on the fringe of Tasman Wilderness Area in Kahurangi National Park. No huts, bridges, signs or aerial access are permitted in a wilderness area, thus trampers must visit on nature's own terms. (DP)

occurrence that inexperienced people descending into the hole become lost, resulting in a dangerous search and rescue mission.

Hunting

Introduced red deer, pigs and goats are present in the park and while recreational hunting is encouraged, there are some restrictions. The whole park is closed to hunting from the third Monday in December to the weekend after Waitangi Day (or in which it falls). Hunting is not allowed near tracks, road-ends and public huts.

Hunting permits are available from Department of Conservation offices. The northern part of the park, north of Awaroa, requires its own

Top tips

- Visit the park during winter. The weather is mild and generally more stable, the crowds are absent, the wildlife still present, the scenery just as stunning.
- Tōtaranui campground offers a traditional, basic New Zealand camping experience (cold showers, no electricity) and is a great base from which to explore some of the best features of the park. Avoid late December and January, when the camp is always fully booked, with a waiting list. (There is poor cellphone coverage at the camp.)
- Awaroa also rates as a great base for park explorations, with the huge estuary, wetlands, Onetahuti Beach and Tonga Island Marine Reserve all within easy reach. Accommodation includes a park hut and campsite, and lodge accommodation.
- Drive into Canaan Downs and walk to the Harwoods Hole lookout for a view of the strange karst landforms.
- Best beach in the park? Onetahuti, the golden link between national park and marine reserve.

hunting permit, which can be obtained from the Golden Bay area office in Tākaka. A separate permit is required for dogs (for pig hunting), and this can be obtained from the relevant area office

Information

Getting there: There are several access points. Marahau, the southern entrance, is 67 km by road from Nelson. From Tākaka Hill (SH60), an 11 km road enters the uplands of the park. From Tākaka (107 km from Nelson) it is 21 km to the northern, Wainui entrance and 32 km to Tōtaranui. Regular bus services run from Nelson and Motueka to Marahau, Wainui and Tōtaranui, water taxis operate along the park's eastern coastline and tramper shuttle services run from the major towns in the region. Helicopter and small plane access is also possible to Awaroa.

When to go: Any time. Summer is particularly popular.

Climate: High sunshine hours, hot summers, mild winters. Annual coastal rainfall of 1800 mm, no rainy season. Slightly colder on the upland areas, with occasional snow during winter.

Accommodation and facilities: There is lodge accommodation at Marahau, Torrent Bay, Anchorage and Awaroa, self-catering accommodation at Torrent Bay, and motel, backpacker and camping accommodation at Marahau and nearby Kaiteriteri. Tōtaranui campground has fireplaces, shelter, toilets, cold showers and laundry facilities, but no power. A small camp office operates over summer, displays explain the park's natural and human history, and there is also a boat ramp and waterski lane.

There are cafés at Awaroa, Marahau and Pōhara. Tākaka and Motueka are the nearest towns, with shops, restaurants, banks, accommodation and visitor centres.

Commercial ventures: Guided sea kayaking trips, kayak hire, guided walks, nature cruises, scuba diving, water taxis, swimming with seals, waka (Māori canoe) trips.

Further reading: Abel Tasman Parkmap; NZMS 260 series topographical maps N25, N26; park brochures and fact sheets.

Visitor centres: The i-SITE visitor centres in Motueka, Golden Bay and Nelson, which includes the Department of Conservation regional visitor centre, offer information, brochures, maps, hut tickets and Abel Tasman Coast Track season passes. Hut tickets can also be booked through Department of Conservation offices and some outdoor stores, campgrounds, hostels, and transport and kayak operators in the region.

Nelson Regional Visitor Centre
79 Trafalgar Street
Nelson
Phone 0-3-546 9339
Email nelsonvc@doc.govt.nz
Open daily
(except Christmas Day)

Golden Bay i-SITE Visitor Centre
Willow Street
Tākaka
Phone 0-3-525 9136
Email gb.vin@NelsonNZ.com
Open daily
(except Christmas Day)

Motueka i-SITE Visitor Centre
20 Wallace St
Motueka
Phone 0-3-528 0005
Email bookings@AbelTasmanGreenrush.co.nz
Open daily (except Christmas Day)

Kahurangi National Park

Location: north-west corner of the South Island

Features: mountains ▪ marble karst landforms ▪ tablelands and downs ▪ vast forests ▪ remote coastline

Activities: short walks ▪ tramping ▪ caving ▪ rafting and kayaking ▪ hunting ▪ fishing

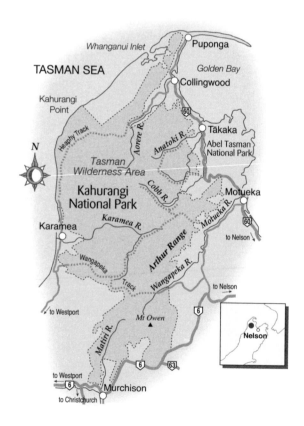

Kahurangi, New Zealand's second largest national park, has some of the most outstanding natural landforms, habitats, and plant and animal communities of any of New Zealand's protected conservation areas.

Visitors are attracted to the park by its marbled mountains and caves and curious fluted rock forms, and by its vast wilderness. The park covers much of the north-west corner of the South Island and extends all the way from alpine tops and tablelands through valleys, lakes and forests to the remote and rugged West Coast. Tramping options range from the historic Heaphy Track, one of New Zealand's Great Walks, to remote routes. Caving, day walks, fishing (for introduced trout) and river rafting are other popular activities.

About the park

Kahurangi's complex geology has a special fascination. Within the park are New Zealand's oldest rocks, fossils and landforms, finest marble karst landscapes and longest, deepest and oldest cave systems. Sedimentary, metamorphic and igneous rock types are all present, as are the influences of glaciation and tectonic movement.

The park is characterised by curiously fluted rock, arches, sinkholes, shafts, caves and disappearing and reappearing streams. The magnificent Mt Owen massif and more readily accessible Mt Arthur are considered outstanding examples of glaciated marble landforms. Mt Owen (1875 m) is the highest peak in the park, though Kahurangi's mountains are not high compared with mountains of the Main Divide to the south.

Mt Owen and Mt Arthur are known as the 'mountains with plumbing'. Water has slowly dissolved the marble to create extensive underground drainage systems that contain their own special ecosystems and have become a drawcard for international speleologists (cavers). The Nettlebed passages under Mt Arthur reach a depth of 889 m, making it the deepest cave system in the Southern Hemisphere. The longest is the Bulmer system beneath Mt Owen, where over 40 km of passages have been surveyed, with plenty yet to explore.

Further west the Honeycomb caves in Oparara Valley, near Karamea, are a treasure chest of sub-fossil bird remains, dating back 20,000 years and including bones of several species that are now extinct, such as the moa. Above ground spectacular marble arches are within easy walking distance from the nearest road-end.

There are more geological curiosities. The Mt Arthur tablelands, Gouland Downs (on the Heaphy Track), Gunner Downs and Matiri Plateau are remnants of ancient peneplains, the oldest landforms in New Zealand. Granites of the park are similar to those in Fiordland, 450 km to the south, because 25 million years ago the two regions were contiguous before lateral earth movement along the South Island's Alpine Fault shifted Fiordland southwards. Glacier-formed landscapes are also a feature of Kahurangi, particularly in the Cobb Valley where there are fine examples of cirque lakes, U-shaped valleys and moraines.

A plethora of flora

The park's geological complexity is the basis of a huge range of natural ecosystems, and plant life is incredibly varied. Growing within Kahurangi are more than half of New Zealand's 2500 native plant species, over 80 per cent of all alpine species, 67 species found nowhere else and 50 species considered rare or endangered.

The park's greatest plant diversity is found on the alpine tops. Because this region largely escaped New Zealand's most recent period of glaciation, it was a major refuge for plants and creatures destroyed by great ice sheets in other areas.

Many of New Zealand's forest types grow in Kahurangi. Beech forests cover the drier, inland valley slopes, lofty podocarps with luxuriant understoreys fill western valleys, and forests of subtropical nature, featuring nīkau palms, tree ferns and kiekie, flourish along the coast. At higher altitudes are subalpine forests of distinctive *Dracophyllum traversii* and mountain cedar.

Wildlife wonders

Kahurangi provides sanctuary for an abundance of animal species, many unique to this region. There are 18 species of native birds, including several threatened species. The park is one of three remaining strongholds in New Zealand of the great spotted kiwi. The large size of the park means it is well suited for birds that range widely, such as South Island kākā, kea and New Zealand falcon. Kākāriki live among the mid-altitude beech forests and rare blue ducks frequent remote, swift-flowing rivers; rock wrens inhabit outcrops above the bushline while fernbirds and ground-foraging weka dwell in western pākihi (swamp) regions. Park visitors are most likely to encounter the more common birds that live in the park, for example the songsters tūī and bellbirds, and sociable South Island robins.

Kahurangi is also a stronghold for half of New Zealand's 40 species of native land snails. These ancient carnivorous creatures, from the *Powelliphanta* genus, have evolved over 80 million years and adapted to a wide range of environments. They shelter from prey during the day and feed at night on worms that grow up to a metre in length.

There is a host of other wildlife in the park: long-tailed and short-tailed bats, four species of gecko, giant wētā and 12 native freshwater fish species. Many of the park's rivers have remained free from introduced trout, an unusual situation in mainland New Zealand today and therefore of special ecological value. Fur seals, little blue penguins and other sea birds live along the park's remote coastline.

Living underground are more rarities: tiny, blind and colourless cave-dwelling invertebrates known as troglobites, and New Zealand's largest native spider – a rare species with a leg span of up to 120 mm.

People in the park

Kahurangi literally means 'blue skies'; it also refers to something noble, or precious, and is indeed a fitting name for this magnificent park. The name derives from Kahurangi Point, in the remote and rugged north-western corner of the park. The point marks the north-western boundary of the Ngāi Tahu tribal area, and is officially classified as a topuni – an overlay of tribal values in recognition of its special significance.

Historically, Kahurangi Point was a landing place for Māori waka (canoes) travelling along the West Coast. It was an easily identified point and provided the only safe haven for a long distance along this wild coastline. The point overlooks Whanganui Inlet, one of New Zealand's largest unmodified estuaries, fringed by primeval rainforest.

During the late 19th and early 20th century, grazing and mining activities, together with hydro-electric power development, had some impact on peripheral areas, but the majority of the park's nearly 500,000 ha remains unmodified. It is nature's own territory.

What to do

Short walks

There are many options for short walks in this huge park. The main choices are in the Cobb Valley (which includes a striking approach by road), on the Mt Arthur tablelands (starting from the Flora road-end), in the Wangapeka Valley, from the West Coast town of Karamea and from Golden Bay. Following is just a selection of the best options; the parkmap and brochures contain a full list and access details.

Mt Arthur Hut (Flora road-end) 1.5 hours one way
A gently graded 6 km path through beech trees, overhanging *Draco-phyllum* and mountain cedar. A short climb beyond the hut is rewarded with great views of Tasman Bay and the Mt Arthur tablelands.

Flora Hut (Flora road-end) 30 minutes one way
A gentle, forested path that follows an old miners' pack track for 2 km to a clearing and Flora Hut, a lovely picnic spot for young families.

Asbestos Cottage (Cobb Valley) 1.5 hours one way

A historic 6 km walk to the ruins of an old asbestos mine and the quaint Asbestos Cottage, where a miner and his wife lived for nearly 40 years and which has now been restored for use as a park hut.

Cobb Dam to Lake Sylvester (Cobb Valley) 2 hours one way

A zigzag climb through beech forest to Sylvester Hut. Lake Sylvester and several other glacial lakes are scattered around this delightful area. Note there are no track markers beyond Lake Sylvester.

Chaffey's Hut (Cobb Valley) 1.5 hours one way

Wander beyond the Cobb Reservoir along a well-defined walking track to derelict Chaffey's Hut. There are swimming, picnic and fishing spots along the way. After the hut the track turns into a tramping track.

Blue Creek Walk (Wangapeka Valley) 1 hour one way

Starting from Courthouse Flat, a gold-mining settlement in the 1880s, this easy walk leads to where Blue Creek emerges from a marble bluff, an example of a subterranean passage in this karst landscape. There are forest clearings and remnants of mining machinery and tailings.

Other walks in the Courthouse Flat vicinity lead to lovely swimming holes (such as Lutine Pool), a view of the park's highest peak, Mt Owen, a river gorge, and old stamping batteries and other mining relics. The forest is a mix of grassy flats, regenerating native vegetation and mature kahikatea and mataī trees.

Nīkau Walk (Karamea) 40 minutes one way

A look at the lush rainforest on the park's coastline. This walk crosses the Kohaihai River by suspension bridge, then wanders through groves of nīkau trees, northern rātā and other coastal vegetation.

Scotts Beach (Karamea) 1 hour one way

The western, coastal end of the Heaphy Track climbs over a small hill (Kohaihai Saddle), through stunted, wind-blown shrublands to Scotts Beach. A great picnic spot on a piece of wild coastline.

Oparara Limestone Arches (Karamea) 40 minutes return

The most impressive and easily accessible of the park's karst limestone formations. Nine kilometres north of Karamea an old logging road climbs into Oparara Basin to a car park. From here a well-formed walking track follows Oparara River to the Oparara Arch, a dramatic, 200 m long, 47 m wide and 37 m high formation. A second, rougher track (1 hour return) leads to a smaller formation, Moria Gate.

Kaituna Track (Golden Bay) 3 hours return

Follows an old gold miners' pack track through magnificent rainforest. Giant northern rātā, pukatea, rimu and beech trees tower over smaller trees, palms, ferns and vines. Bird life thrives here. Added interest is provided by the old gold workings of the Kaituna goldfield, never a highly productive field despite being worked for some 40 years. A rougher tramping route continues beyond the goldfield to Knuckle Hill and the north-west corner of the park.

Longer walks

Again, the following is a very small selection of a great range of opportunities.

Mt Arthur (Flora road-end) 8 hours return

A close look at the distinctive karst rock of Mt Arthur, with the bonus of great views. The poled route continues uphill from Mt Arthur Hut. Pick a good day and take care around the bluffs, sinkholes and caves. The route is above the bushline and exposed, and weather can change quickly. In winter the mountain will be snow-covered and climbing experience and equipment is required.

Fenella Hut (Cobb Valley) 4 to 5 hours one way

Cobb Valley is a classic, glacier-formed U-shaped valley, featuring several small glacial lakes, beech forest, tussock clearings and subalpine herbfields. A good walking track for the first hour leads past great swimming and fishing spots in the Cobb River, then a more basic tramping track continues up the wide valley floor, through beech forest and tussock clearings, to the tiny Cobb Hut (4 bunks). A side trip here leads to Cobb Lake and Round Lake. From Cobb Hut the track climbs rocky terrain above the bushline to Fenella Hut. It's a delightful base for exploring the small glacial lakes and nearby peaks and, for those with suitable tramping experience, more challenging marked and unmarked routes that lead into remote areas of the park.

Lake Matiri (Matiri Road) 2 hours one way

In the very south-eastern corner of the park a tramping track climbs an old pack track to this forest-surrounded lake that was formed during the 1929 Murchison earthquake, when rockfalls damned the Matiri River. The West Matiri River can rise quickly in wet weather and be difficult to cross. Native wetland birds living on the lake include paradise shelducks, scaups, grey ducks and little shags. (From the lake a track leads further up Matiri Valley, and a poled route turns off and climbs to the park's tussock- and herb-covered Thousand Acre Plateau.)

Multi-day tramping trips

Mt Arthur Tablelands Circuit 2 days

Regarded as an excellent introduction to tramping in Kahurangi. From the Flora road-end car park, the Flora Track, an old pack track, leads to Flora Hut then Salisbury Track continues through a forested valley and climbs gently to Salisbury Lodge (24 bunks) on the tussock-covered Mt Arthur tablelands. Three old rock shelters along the way also provide accommodation. For experienced trampers a return circuit to the car park is possible via Gordons Pyramid and along a narrow ridge, past sinkholes and marble outcrops, beneath Mt Arthur.

Another option for more experienced trampers is to follow a poled route from Salisbury Lodge across the tablelands to Balloon Hut, then skirt beneath Mt Peel to Lake Peel and descend to the Cobb Valley.

A longer (3 day) circuit is possible by climbing back up from the Cobb Valley via Bullock and Upper Tākaka Tracks and returning to the Flora road-end.

Heaphy Track 4 to 6 days

One of New Zealand's oldest, longest and most popular tramping trips. Māori followed this route to the coast for hundreds of years, gold prospectors developed it further in the late 19th century, and the first Heaphy Hut was built in 1907. Today some 5000 people each year walk the track, traversing its interesting diversity of landscapes: beech forests and rainforests, tussock-covered downs, limestone arches, river valleys and remote, windswept coastline. The Gouland Downs area of the track is one of the last strongholds for the great spotted kiwi. Other special animals that could be encountered include *Powelliphanta*, a carnivorous native land snail, and long-tailed bats, sometimes seen feeding at dusk in the Heaphy Valley.

The 82 km track is wide and benched over most of its length. There are seven huts, with bunks, heating, water and toilets, and all except Brown and Gouland Downs have gas cookers. There are also nine campsites with water supply and toilets. Huts and campsites must be booked, check the Department of Conservation website for details. There is a two-night limit on staying at each hut.

The northern track end is in Golden Bay, 28 km from Collingwood and the southern end is on the West Coast, 15 minutes from Karamea. Bus and taxi services are available to each end of the track from these towns, and regular bus services link Westport and Nelson. Chartered air services are available to return walkers to their starting point. Air services are also available to Golden Bay from Auckland and Wellington. Telephone services have been installed at both track ends, and local calls requesting transport are free.

Note that heavy rain can occur suddenly on the track and small streams can become dangerous to cross. The open downs are exposed to cold winds and rain. There is a high-tide track for when the beach is impassable near Crayfish Point. Tide times are posted in the two nearest huts.

Wangapeka Track 4 to 6 days

Traverses the park from east to west along four beech-forested valleys and over two subalpine passes, following parts of a pack track built during gold rush days of the late 19th century. Farming attempts in the Wangapeka Valley in the 19th century were abandoned when introduced deer provided too much competition for feed. After much of the track was destroyed by the 1929 Murchison earthquake, it was rebuilt by workers during the 1930s Depression. Cecil King's restored historic hut, 3.5 hours up the Wangapeka, is a legacy of these tenacious track builders, miners and farmers. King spent every summer of his 20-year retirement in the valley fossicking for gold, until he died in 1982.

Top tips

- Walk the Heaphy Track – the diverse landscapes and history make it one of New Zealand's outstanding tramping tracks.
- For a gentle introduction to tramping in a magnificent mountain landscape, head to the Mt Arthur tablelands – in summer, with a good weather forecast.
- There's heaps of family fun to be enjoyed in the Cobb Valley: great campsites, rivers and a reservoir for swimming, boating and fishing, and delightful, easy short walks in surrounding forests.
- Stay overnight in one of the rock shelters on the Mt Arthur tablelands. An exciting adventure for young families. Mt Arthur and Flora Hut are also within very easy reach.
- Visit Oparara Arch, an outstanding limestone karst landform in the 'marbled park'.
- Make your way to the little-visited north-west corner of the park, reached through Golden Bay. Knuckle Hill provides a stunning outlook of the park, the Whanganui Inlet marine reserve and wildlife management reserve, and the amazing sand expanse of Farewell Spit, a world-recognised bird sanctuary.

There are five huts, plus Cecil King's 4-bunk slab hut and two shelters, along the 52 km track. There are also several good campsites. Major and most minor rivers have bridges or three-wire crossings, and alternative tracks are available where rivers can flood the lower track. A bus service is available from Nelson to Tapawera. Shuttle services can be chartered to each end of the track from Nelson, Motueka and Tapawera (eastern side) and Karamea (western side). There are public phones at each end of the track. An air service can be chartered to transport trampers between Karamea and Nelson.

The track can be walked in conjunction with the Leslie/Karamea Track to the Mt Arthur tablelands, or the Heaphy Track, to create circuits between the West Coast and Nelson sides of the park.

Leslie–Karamea Track 6 to 9 days

A rugged, wilderness tramping track through the remote, central region of the park that links the Mt Arthur tablelands with the Wangapeka Track. The track is marked but not benched and quite rough in places. Many streams are not bridged, and water levels can rise quickly and cause delays. Streams and rivers should not be crossed when in flood.

The track follows the upper Leslie and Karamea Valleys, through a mix of beech and podocarp forest and open river flats. Slips and a lake, dammed by a huge rockfall, are reminders of past earthquakes. Less common park birds, kākā and kākāriki, are likely companions.

There are five huts, one natural rock shelter that sleeps eight comfortably, and several delightful campsites.

Tasman Wilderness Area

In the heart of the park is a 87,000 ha wilderness area of valleys, lakes, gorges and mountains. There are no huts, tracks, bridges or signs and no air access, presenting unlimited tramping opportunities for those willing and able to travel self-sufficiently. This area is centred on the Tasman Mountains and mid-Karamea valley. Roaring Lion Hut, in the remote heart of the park, is the closest hut to the wilderness area.

Wilderness areas

In wildness is the preservation of the world.

These words of American conservationist Henry Thoreau have universal appeal. And while people's concept of wilderness can vary significantly – one person's crowded tourist track is another person's wild isolation – there is enshrined in New Zealand conservation legislation a special classification and protection for remote natural areas that can truly be classified as 'wilderness'.

Criteria for wilderness areas include being large enough to take at least two days' foot travel to traverse, having no facilities such as huts, tracks, bridges or signs, and allowing no aerial access. There must also be significant 'buffer zones' to protect the core wilderness areas.

While wilderness areas are principally a recreational concept, their special designation is obviously compatible with nature conservation. They preserve indigenous biodiversity and natural features, and for people who explore them they foster self-reliance, challenge, discovery, solitude, freedom and empathy with nature.

Each wilderness area encompasses tens of thousands of hectares of remote country: mountains, forests, rivers, glaciers, snowfields and ice plateaus. They include Tasman (Kahurangi National Park), Adams (Westland/Tai Poutini National Park), Paparoa (just north of Paparoa National Park), Pembroke and Glasinock (both Fiordland National Park), Hooker/Landsborough (south of Aoraki/Mt Cook National Park), Olivine (Mt Aspiring National Park) and Raukumara (Raukumara Forest Park, north-east of Te Urewera National Park).

With the wild lands of the world rapidly diminishing, the opportunities these New Zealand wilderness areas offer are of increasing international significance.

Caving

The deepest and longest caving systems are found beneath the Owen massif and the Arthur Range. These under-mountain marble worlds are strictly for those with suitable experience.

The limestone arches of the Oparara River (see p106) and the Honeycomb Hill cave system are more accessible. Because of the presence of sub-fossil bird remains dating back 20,000 years and including bones of extinct species such as moa and giant eagle, these caves are protected and access is restricted to guided tours only.

Boating/rafting

Cobb Reservoir, in Cobb Valley, is popular for kayaking and sailing (power boats are prohibited). The Karamea is a challenging whitewater rafting or kayaking river, highly regarded for its wilderness qualities. Whitewater rafting trips are available.

Fishing

Introduced brown trout are present in all major rivers throughout the park. The Wangapeka and Karamea in particular are recognised as outstanding brown trout fisheries. The Cobb Reservoir and feeding rivers are popular rainbow and brown trout fisheries. The reservoir is open for fishing all year, though rivers in the park are closed during the winter. Fishing guides are available, and fishing licences are obtainable from the Fish and Game Council (www.fishandgame.org.nz).

Hunting

Recreational hunting of introduced red deer, fallow deer, pigs and goats is encouraged in the park, though no hunting is permitted within

1 km of the Heaphy Track. Hunting permits are required, and these are available from Department of Conservation offices.

Information

Getting there: Nelson, the nearest city, is served by daily road and air services. From Nelson drive west on SH60 or south-west on SH6 to reach the park. Roads lead to the park from Motueka, Tākaka, Murchison and Karamea (some are steep, unsealed and subject to flooding or snow). There are air services to Motueka, Tākaka and Karamea. Air and road transport services operate for the Heaphy and Wangapeka Tracks.

When to go: Any time, though there will be snow in winter.

Climate: Generally milder than more southern parks, but temperatures vary. Snow can fall throughout the year but only the highest levels are snowbound in winter. Inland, heavy frosts are frequent in winter. Heavy rainfall (up to 5600 mm a year). As with most mountain climes, weather can be unpredictable and subject to sudden changes.

Accommodation and facilities: There is a wide range of accommodation in the Nelson region and in towns around the park, including luxury lodges, hotels, motels, bed-and-breakfasts, backpacker hostels, camping grounds with campervan sites. There are shops, supermarkets, restaurants, banks, fuel and other services in Nelson (especially cafés!) and in the towns surrounding the park.

Within the park there are camping and picnic areas and some 50 huts and shelters. Camping is permitted, except for along the Heaphy Track where it is restricted to designated campsites. There is a network of 570 km of walking tracks and tramping tracks throughout the park.

Commercial ventures: Walking, fishing, hunting guides are available, also whitewater rafting tours on the Karamea and cave tours at the Honeycomb caves, from Karamea.

Further reading: Kahurangi Parkmap; NZMS 260 series topographical maps M26, M27, M28, L27, L28; park brochures and fact sheets.

Special conditions: Weather in the park can be very changeable, particularly at high altitudes. Always carry warm clothing and wet-weather gear and make sure your experience matches the trip you are contemplating. On some tracks where there are no bridges, river levels can rise quickly and cause delays. Be patient: it's better to wait another night in safety than risk a hasty and dangerous crossing.

Visitor centres: Visitor information centres in Nelson, Motueka, Golden Bay, Karamea, Westport and Murchison (summer only) all provide information and advice about the park, plus maps, brochures, hut tickets and bookings for commercial operators. Most are open seven days a week. Hunting permits are available from Department of Conservation offices in the area in which you wish to hunt. There are offices in Westport, Motueka, Golden Bay.

Nelson Regional Visitor Centre
79 Trafalgar Street
Nelson
Phone 0-3-546 9339
Email nelsonvc@doc.govt.nz

Westport i-SITE Visitor Centre
1 Brougham Street
Westport
Phone 0-3-789 6658
Email westport.info@xtra.co.nz

Karamea Information and
Resource Centre
Market Cross
PO Box 94
Karamea
Phone 0-3-782 6652

Motueka i-SITE Visitor Centre
20 Wallace St
Motueka
Phone 0-3-528 0005
Email bookings@
AbelTasmanGreenrush.co.nz

Murchison Information Centre
47 Waller Street
Murchison
Phone 0-3-523 9350
Email murchinfo@xtra.co.nz

Golden Bay i-SITE Visitor Centre
Willow Street
Tākaka
Phone 0-3-525 9136
Email gb.vin@NelsonNZ.com

Paparoa
National Park

Location: South Island West Coast

Features: canyons, caves and blowholes ▪ forest diversity from mountain ranges to the sea

Activities: short walks ▪ tramping ▪ river kayaking ▪ caving ▪ birdwatching

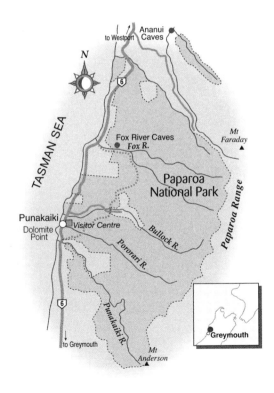

Intriguing limestone formations and a great diversity of forest types and bird life are the major features of Paparoa. One of New Zealand's smallest national parks, Paparoa has been established with carefully chosen boundaries to safeguard complete ecosystems extending from the mountain ranges to the coast.

Paparoa's coastline is a visual treat for travellers on the scenic West Coast highway. Sculptured cliffs and caves, covered by hardy coastal shrubs, northern rātā trees and nīkau palms, typify this weather- and water-blasted coast. The best known of several delightful coastal short walks is to the pancake rocks and blowholes at Punakaiki.

Inland, there are densely forested limestone canyons, while below ground level there lies an elaborate network of shafts, passages and caves.

Most visitors to Paparoa explore the short walks; others head inland to kayak the river canyons or explore the one major tramping track. The hidden cave systems attract specialist speleologists, while guided cave tours provide an option for those with less knowledge and ability. Birdwatching is also popular, given the range of native sea birds and bush birds that live in and around the park.

About the park

Paparoa is one of New Zealand's newest national parks, created in 1987 after a major logging proposal for the West Coast forests prompted a vigorous conservation campaign.

The park lies between the ancient, weathered crest of the Paparoa Range and the cliffs and coves of the coastline. The varied forest types and microclimates, the altitudinal range and the high-fertility limestone ecosystems have created a huge diversity of natural habitats. The park's forests and coastline support the highest concentration of native birds recorded in New Zealand and, in the limestone basin alone, botanists have identified at least 25 distinct forest communities.

Of karst, caves and old rock

Linking the mountains with the sea is a low-lying, forested limestone basin filled with canyons, caves, fluted rock, sinkholes and disappearing streams, such as those easily explored in the Pororari and Fox River valleys. The effects of water, over time, have dissolved the soft limestone and created this peculiar landscape, which is known as karst.

Organised caving groups have explored and mapped caves throughout the park's limestone basin. Many of these are storehouses for important fossil material of birds, reptiles and even mammals. Bird-bone deposits have been found in the Ananui Cave; the adjoining Tiropahi system contains fossil whale deposits; and the 5 km Xanadu system is known for its ever-changing water levels.

On the eastern side of the park, limestone gives way to old granite and gneiss rock in the Paparoa Range. These mountains, which reach a height of 1500 m, are made of the most ancient rocks known in New Zealand. The rocks bear close resemblance to Fiordland's because they were once aligned with the Fiordland mountains, before being separated by the Alpine Fault within the last 10 million years. The jumble of craggy peaks and pinnacles, glaciated hanging valleys, bluffs and cirques are untracked and often covered in dense cloud, presenting a formidable challenge to trampers.

Subtropical forests

Paparoa's moist and temperate coastal climate has produced a luxuriant covering of subtropical lowland rainforest. The limestone basin is covered with dense forest of podocarps, red beech, broadleafs and tree ferns. On the coast, nīkau palms and northern rātā thrive, near the southern limits of their distribution, among entanglements of kiekie and vines, and dense wind-shorn shrublands of flax and cabbage trees survive the battle with salt-laden wind.

In the wetter, cooler montane climate of the Paparoa Range, silver beech forest merges with subalpine shrubs of *Dracophyllum*, pink pine and mountain flax. Higher still, *Celmisia* daisies and gentians survive among golden snow tussock and *Olearia* shrubs. In the north of the park, pākihi (swamps) on old terraces of the Tiropahi River add yet more floral diversity.

Special species

The endemic Westland petrel breeds only on the Punakaiki coast and is one of the few mainland petrel colonies to have survived the introduction of rats, cats and stoats. These petrels live at sea except for during their winter breeding season, when couples raise their chicks in burrows on coastal terraces, and take off for their daily feeding flights from exposed rocks or trees. Watching thousands fly in at dusk is a memorable sight.

The park's other noteworthy bird is the great spotted kiwi, roroa. Paparoa is one of only two areas where this species is relatively abundant.

What to do

Short walks

Pancake Rocks and Blowholes (Punakaiki) 20 minutes loop

This is the most-visited short walk in all of New Zealand's national parks. The main attractions are the pancake rocks – extraordinary layered limestone stacks – and the spectacle that occurs as sea swells surge against them and erupt in geyser-like explosions from chasms and collapsed sea caverns. Even on a calm day the walk is stunning. The pancake rocks, sea chambers and cliffs are always impressive, there is a variety of coastal forest, including hardy plants clinging to the cliffs, while sea birds – shags, white-fronted terns and gulls – will be likely companions. Looking seaward, Hector's dolphins (the world's smallest dolphins) might be playing in the swells. On a clear day the soaring peak of Aoraki/Mt Cook, New Zealand's highest mountain, can be seen in the distance. The path is enhanced by stylish interpretative signs. It is suitable for wheelchair users, with assistance.

Pororari River (Punakaiki) 2.5 hours return

A look at one of the deep river canyons in the park, this gently graded track starts by the coast highway near Punakaiki and follows the river inland to a stunning gorge. Deep pools, huge boulders and lots of easy access to the river for swimming (when not in flood) are also river features, while the forest changes subtly from subtropical to temperate as you move inland.

Truman Track (SH6 north of Punakaiki) 15 minutes return

A short walk through subtropical forest, then a staircase descent to a rocky beach backed by cliffs, caverns, a blowhole and plunging waterfall, all of which typify the Paparoa coastline. A visit timed during low tide will allow exploration of the beach. The forest features rimu, mataī and northern rātā trees, emerging above a tangle of vines and nīkau palms, then changes to hardy flaxes, coastal shrubs and matted herbs on the sea facing cliffs.

Fox River Cave (SH6 north of Punakaiki) 2.5 hours return

Signposted as the 'Tourist Cave', as people have been visiting this cave since the late 19th century. From the coast highway the walk first follows the Inland Pack Track, then continues on the same side of the river after the Inland Pack Track crosses a ford. Take torches with spare batteries for your exploration of the cave, with its 200 m passage and stunning calcite formations. There is a second, lower cave, which is dangerous to enter unless you are experienced and equipped with specialist caving equipment to negotiate the sheer drops and falling rocks.

The Fox River also showcases some fine limestone formations – canyons, sculptured rock pools and disappearing streams.

Multi-day tramping trip

Inland Pack Track 2 days

The only formed tramping track in the park, the Inland Pack Track follows a historic route and explores many outstanding limestone and forest features north of Punakaiki. The 27 km track was originally formed in the 1860s during the West Coast gold rush days as a safer alternative to the rugged and treacherous coastline route. A section of cobbling still intact is testament to the stone-building skills of the miners who constructed the route. The gently graded track leads through the heart of the park's limestone basin, meandering beneath limestone escarpments, across deep chasms and among potholes and sinkholes. For safety, it is best to stay on the track.

Adding a third day to your trip will allow time to explore several interesting side trips. Alternatively, the track can be walked as separate half or full day trips by linking with two coastal tracks. There are no huts but there is a unique 'sheltered camping' option at the Ballroom, a huge limestone overhang, as well as other pleasant camping spots at Bullock Creek Farm and the Fossil/Dilemma Creek junction. Note there are four major rivers to cross by ford and much creekbed travel. Water levels can rise suddenly. Check weather conditions first at the park visitor centre and when on the track, if in doubt, don't cross. Walking in a northerly direction is recommended.

Caving

The karst limestone of the park offers caving opportunities to suit all abilities, from the curious novice to very experienced caver. The Fox River Cave, with its 200 m passage and stunning calcite formations, is a historic tourist attraction. An even more easily visited cave is the Punakaiki Cavern, beside the main highway at Punakaiki, which features 130 m of passages and occasional glow worms.

Visiting other caves in the park requires the expertise of experienced speleologists. New Zealand caving groups have explored and mapped caves throughout the park's limestone basin.

Birdwatching

The only breeding colony of the endemic Westland petrel is just south of the park, and the spectacle of hundreds of these birds flying in after a day's fishing is remarkable. Visits to the colony can be prearranged during the breeding season, between April and November.

In the park itself, venture onto any tracks around dawn or dusk and the resident native bird life will make its prolific presence known.

Kayaking

Gentle and very scenic kayaking is popular in the Pororari River gorge. Kayaks can be hired at Punakaiki.

Top tips

- The Pancake Rocks and Blowholes Walk at Punakaiki is a must. The best chance of seeing the blowholes working is by visiting around high tide – though the sight is dramatic in any conditions.
- Explore Truman Track at low tide. This allows access along the interesting beach at the end of the track.
- If visiting in summer, look for splashes of red-flowering rātā. The species here is northern rātā, growing at its southernmost limit. Some flowering seasons are particularly spectacular.
- Take an easy meander along Pororari River Walk into one of the park's river canyons.
- A longer but rewarding walk is to the Fox River Cave. The cave's 200 m passage is decorated with limestone formations.

Fishing

Introduced brown trout live in the rivers in the park. Fishing licences are not available at Punakaiki so must be organised before your visit. They are available in Greymouth and Westport, or online at www. fishandgame.org.nz.

Hunting

Introduced goats live in the park. Hunting permits are available from Department of Conservation offices.

Information

Getting there: By road via SH6, 57 km from Westport and 47 km from Greymouth. There are airports at Westport and Hokitika (41 km south of Greymouth). Daily bus services are available.

When to go: Any time, though the most settled weather is from January to April, and in mid winter.

Climate: Mild and wet, with some periods of settled weather. Rainfall varies from 8000 mm per year inland to 2000 mm on the coast.

Accommodation and facilities: At Punakaiki there are cafés, craft shops, a tavern and accommodation including a four-star hotel, motel, campground (with cabins), backpacker hostel and several self-catering cottages and bed-and-breakfast choices. Westport and Greymouth are fully serviced towns with supermarkets, banks and accommodation. The nearest fuel is at Westport or at Rūnanga (35 km south of Punakaiki).

Commercial ventures: Guided caving tours, guided kayak trips and kayak hire, natural heritage tours, tramper shuttle service, Westland petrel tours (by prior arrangement).

Further reading: Paparoa Parkmap; NZMS 260 series topographical map K30; park brochures.

Special conditions: The limestone country in the park is filled with hidden potholes and shafts. Keep to the tracks. Torches are necessary for exploring caves.

Inland tramping tracks involve river crossings and streambed travel. Choose fording spots carefully and do not attempt to negotiate flooded rivers. Never underestimate how quickly weather conditions can change and how fast river levels can rise. Check the weather forecast and conditions at the park visitor centre before walking in the park.

On coastal tracks be wary of tidal changes, keep behind clifftop barriers and follow the advice on signs.

Visitor centre: Paparoa National Park Visitor Centre offers information on walks, tracks, weather, caving and commercial services, plus maps, brochures and other conservation products for sale, displays and a superb 15-minute audiovisual. Located on SH6 at Punakaiki, opposite the entrance to the pancake rocks.

Paparoa National Park Visitor Centre
PO Box 1
Punakaiki
Phone 0-3-731 1895
Email punakaikivc@doc.govt.nz
Open daily 8.30 am to 6 pm (summer); 9 am to 4.30 pm (winter)

Arthur's Pass National Park

Location: Southern Alps/Kā Tiritiri o te Moana, central South Island

Features: alpine pass ■ mountains ■ beech forests ■ rainforests ■ river valleys and easily accessible alpine valleys

Activities: walks ■ tramping ■ mountaineering ■ skiing ■ scenic and historic road and railway ■ hunting

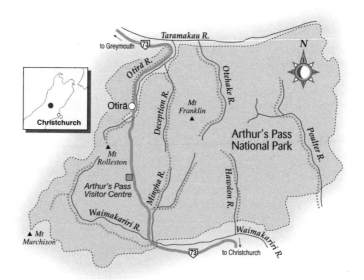

The essence of Arthur's Pass National Park is its mountains, beech forests, rainforests and a history of transport that today allows access to the park's heart. The historic highway that bisects the park and crosses the Main Divide is the highest of the few passes where roads have been built over the Southern Alps/Kā Tiritiri o te Moana.

Visitors can penetrate the heart of the park in comfort, by car or by train. Short walking tracks from the Arthur's Pass highway showcase the park's best features. There is no need for extended exertion to witness the splendour of the mountain peaks, the power of waterfalls and rockslides, the delicacy of alpine flowers, or the cheeky approaches of kea.

Nevertheless there is more to the park than can be seen from the highway. Long valleys and low passes provide natural tramping routes, alpine passes and mountains provide serious climbing challenges, and skiing has long been a tradition in and around the park.

About the park

As with most other South Island national parks, Arthur's Pass has been shaped over the past two million years by the three powerful natural forces of tectonic uplift, glaciation and erosion. The mountains have been forced upwards by the collision of two of the earth's crustal plates, glaciers have gouged U-shaped valleys and the brittle greywacke rock has been severely eroded by water. Ten small glaciers remain high in the park's mountains. They are but tiny remnants of earlier giants that extended west almost to the coast and east to the Canterbury Plains.

The ongoing process of erosion means massive rock avalanches are a feature of the park's landscape. One example can be seen from the road at the head of Otirā Gorge, and the biggest in the park, named Falling Mountain, fills 3 km of riverbed in the remote upper Otehake River. This avalanche occurred as a result of a major earthquake in 1929. Evidence of erosion – steep scree slopes, shingle fans, crumbling ridges and shingle-filled rivers – is found throughout the park. One of the park's major rivers, the Waimakariri, is estimated to at one point have a gravel bed some 300 m deep.

As this alpine park straddles the South Island Main Divide the contrasting east-west climates and changing altitudes result in distinctive physical contrasts and a huge variety of natural habitats.

On the western side, where moist, westerly weather systems prevail, deeply gorged rivers flow through dense rainforests filled with tall podocarps, southern rātā and kāmahi and understorey trees, ferns and vines. On the rain-shadowed eastern side of the Alps, wide, shingle-filled riverbeds are flanked by beech forests. In the mountains between these east and west regions is an alpine wonderland of snow-covered peaks, remnant glaciers, huge scree slopes and, within easy walking distance from the highway, tussockfields, tarns and alpine meadows filled with flowers.

The varied habitats support a great range of native wildlife species, including a particularly diverse invertebrate fauna population. Kea, mischievous mountain parrots, are regular roadside entertainers. Their bush cousins South Island kākā make their presence known by screeching loudly from high above the treetops. Blue ducks live in remote mountain streams while the open braided rivers of the eastern side of the park provide nesting grounds for migrant birds such as the wrybill and black-fronted tern. Great spotted kiwi live on both sides of the Main Divide; their calls can sometimes be heard around Arthur's Pass village and throughout the upper Bealey Valley. Common forest birds in the park include the bellbird, fantail, South Island robin, South Island tit and grey warbler. Less common are yellow-crowned and very rare orange-fronted parakeets (kākāriki) and threatened yellowheads.

The Arthur's Pass Highway is a high and historic highway. Several notable engineering feats mark this road's construction through the steep, erosion-prone mountains, not least its initial completion back in 1866. Construction of the Otira Tunnel in 1923 united the east and west coasts and, in the latest engineering achievement in 1999, a 400 m viaduct was built to minimise the hazards of floods and slips.

Leonard Cockayne, one of New Zealand's most eminent ecologists, helped generate awareness of the region's natural values in the early 20th century when he lived and studied botany at Kellys Creek, just west of Arthur's Pass. Cockayne encouraged the government to legally protect the forests. Two reserves were set aside in 1901 and, in 1929, Arthur's Pass became the first national park in the South Island.

What to do

Short walks

Devils Punchbowl (Arthur's Pass village) 1 hour return
A popular, high-quality walking track, steep in places, through rocky beech forest to a 131 m waterfall. The walking track crosses the Bealey River then climbs wooden steps to the base of the falls.

Bridal Veil Walk (Arthur's Pass village) 1.5 hours return
This walk crosses the Bealey River then follows a gentle gradient through beech forest alongside the river, except for a short, steep pitch as it crosses Bridal Veil Creek. There's a good view looking back to Arthur's Pass village. The track emerges on the highway about 3 km from the village and close to Jack's Hut, a restored roadman's cottage. Information panels in the hut describe the challenges involved in building and maintaining the road over this mountain pass.

Dobson Nature Walk (Arthur's Pass summit) 30 minutes return
One of the most accessible spots in the country to enjoy subalpine and alpine flowers. The gently graded walking track meanders through a delightful range of herbs, tussocks, shrubs and wetland plants, surrounded by the park's biggest mountains. The best flowering time is from November to February. Look for *Celmisia* daisies, mountain violets, buttercups, gentians and hebes. A booklet available from the

park visitor centre helps with plant identification, and information panels on the walk describe the vegetation, geology, and Māori and road-building history.

A longer walk continues through tall red and silver tussock and alpine bogs to connect with the Otirā Valley walking track, about 1 km further along the highway.

Otirā Valley (Arthur's Pass summit) 2 hours return

A delightful wander along this open tussock valley, with mountains on either side, to a footbridge that crosses the rocky headwaters of the Otirā River. Summer flowers are an added bonus. Note an unmarked route continues beyond the bridge giving access to the valley head. This climbs boulders and scree slopes and is prone to rockfalls and, in winter and spring, avalanches.

Temple Basin (Arthur's Pass summit) 1.5 hours one way

Incorporates the access road to Temple Basin ski field, and zigzags uphill beneath mountain bluffs to some great mountain views, finishing at the ski-field buildings. In good weather and when there is no snow it is possible to continue uphill beside the ski tow to reach a benched track around an alpine basin of summer-flowering alpine plants to more mountain and valley views. The additional walk will add a further 3 hours to your trip. The flowers are especially prolific in late spring. Tiny rock wrens might join you on your walk.

Cockayne Nature Walk (Kellys Creek) 30 minutes loop

A gentle climb then descent through southern rātā forest behind a delightful park campsite. This walk commemorates Leonard Cockayne, one of New Zealand's most eminent ecologists, who worked at Kellys Creek in the early 20th century and was instrumental in gaining national park protection for Arthur's Pass. Kākā, fossicking for food among the tree trunks and branches, are likely feathered companions on this walk. In summer, chances are the forest will be emblazoned with red patches courtesy of southern rātā flowers. Some flowering years are better than others.

Above: Pancake Rocks and blowholes at Punakaiki, Paparoa National Park; a short walk to a stunning vista. (SB) Below: looking into Fox River gorge, Paparoa National Park. (SB)

Opposite top: Mt Bovis in Paparoa National Park, one of the more accessible points of the rugged Paparoa Range. (SB)

Opposite bottom: Visitors to alpine parks such as Arthur's Pass are likely to encounter the bold, curious kea, a mountain parrot. (DH)

Above: Waimakariri, a popular tramping valley in Arthur's Pass National Park. (SB)

Right: Lake Mavis, a worthwhile side trip near Goat Pass on the Mingha–Deception route, Arthur's Pass National Park. (SB)

Opposite top: A winter approach to Barker Hut, Arthur's Pass National Park. (SB)

Opposite bottom: Bealey Spur provides steep but relatively short access to the mountain tops near Arthur's Pass village. (SB)

Right: South Island edelweiss. Summer-flowering alpine plants grow beside the highway near Arthur's Pass. (SB)

Below: Reflections, Godley Valley, Aoraki/Mt Cook National Park. (SB)

Left: Aoraki/Mt Cook (3754 m), New Zealand's highest mountain. Looking up the Hooker Valley. (SB)

Below: Main Divide mountains Douglas (left) and Haidinger, bordering Aoraki/Mt Cook and Westland/Tai Poutini National Parks. (SB)

Opposite top left: Frost on a mountain buttercup (*Ranunculus lyallii*), commonly misnamed the Mt Cook lily. (SB)

Opposite top right: Meltwater at the terminus of Fox Glacier in Westland/Tai Poutini National Park. (DP)

Opposite bottom: Peter's Pool, named after famous climbing guide Peter Graham. One of many delightful family walks in Westland/Tai Poutini National Park. (SB)

Karangarua headwaters. Climbing in Westland/Tai Poutini National Park involves arduous and often difficult approaches. (SB)

Longer walks

Avalanche Peak (Arthur's Pass village) 6 to 8 hours return

A steep climb to Avalanche Peak (1833 m) and the open tops above the village. Not for the faint-hearted. Two tracks to Avalanche Peak make a round trip possible. Scott's Track is a longer and more gradual climb, while Avalanche Peak Track is steeper and more direct. Both reward with stunning mountain and glacier views. Kea are likely to be present. Note these walks should only be attempted in good weather. In winter, snow-filled basins around Avalanche Peak are prone to avalanching. A shorter option is to walk to the bushline on Scott's Track, an excellent vantage point. Check the weather conditions at the visitor centre before leaving.

Bealey Spur (Cloudesley Road) 4 to 5 hours return

Another climb to the bushline, through mountain beech then subalpine shrubs and tussock, past tarns, to an old musterer's hut now available as a park hut. The subalpine shrubs have recovered since the area was burnt for grazing in the early 20th century and the climb rewards with views of mountains and the broad flats of the Waimakariri River. The track is on the eastern side of the park and just beyond the rain shadow of the Main Divide, so the weather can be fine here while the rain is pouring at Arthur's Pass, 15 km to the west.

Multi-day tramping trips

The plethora of tramping routes in the park are highly variable in terms of difficulty. They also vary between summer and winter, when many passes are snow-covered and can become mountaineering challenges. No tracks are continuously marked, and most require you to cross unbridged rivers that can rise quickly in heavy rain. Following is a selection of the most popular easy-to-medium tramping trips. A full list and details are available from the park visitor centre.

Avalanche Peak–Crow Valley–Waimakariri Valley 2 days

Features open tops, great views, a downhill scree run, beech forest and some valley travel. It requires good weather for the section over the tops. The route starts by climbing from Arthur's Pass village to Avalanche Peak, then descends a long shingle scree to the Crow Valley. Crow Hut is at the head of the valley. The trip continues by following Crow River (one crossing necessary) to where it meets the Waimakariri River, and follows the river flats to the highway at Klondyke Corner.

Casey Saddle to Binser Saddle Circuit 2 to 3 days

The good things about this round trip are that there are no rivers to ford and only two low alpine passes to cross, and being on the eastern side of the mountains there is a better chance of fine weather. Walking clockwise, the trip starts from the Waimakariri River and heads through beech forest and grassy flats up Andrews Stream. After crossing Casey Saddle (780 m) the track descends to Casey Hut, beside the Poulter, one of the park's major rivers. The circuit then heads down the Poulter River, which is mostly easy walking in the wide, open valley, then climbs gently up Pete Stream, over the forested Binser Saddle (1110 m) and descends to the Waimakariri River. There are two huts as well as ample camping spots.

Kelly Range 2 days

This climbs from the Kellys Creek camping area to the rolling tussock tops of the Kelly Range and Carroll Hut. This is the westernmost range in the park and views extend across the broad Taramakau Valley to the West Coast. Good weather with good visibility is a must, and the range will be snow-covered in winter. For experienced trampers a long multi-day trip is possible from the Kelly Range encompassing the remote Taipō Valley, Harman Pass (1330 m) and Waimakariri Valley.

Mingha–Deception Valleys 2 to 3 days

A popular tramping trip that has become well known in recent years as the run section of the annual Coast to Coast multisport endurance event. At a more sedate pace, trampers can take in the rainforests of

Coast to Coast

A major event that sweeps through the park each year is the Coast to Coast multisport endurance race, which crosses the entire South Island in one or two days. The race involves cycling from the West Coast to Deception River, running the Deception–Mingha Valleys to Klondyke Corner (normally a 2 day tramping trip), kayaking the Waimakariri River then cycling to Sumner on the east coast. The event attracts hundreds of competitors, both individuals and teams, and a host of supporters. Park staff work closely with event organisers to ensure minimal environmental impact in the park. The Coast to Coast is usually held over a weekend in February – either a good time to visit the park or stay well away, depending on your point of view!

Deception Valley, on the western side of the Main Divide, which contrast with the drier eastern beech forests in the Mingha Valley. There is also a chance of spotting blue ducks; small numbers of this endangered bird live in these mountain rivers. The river travel involves lots of crossings and boulder-hopping, but crossing Goat Pass (1070 m) between the valleys is relatively straightforward. There are two huts. A 1 day side trip from Goat Pass to Lake Mavis is well worthwhile.

Harper Pass 5 days
Follows an old trail travelled by early Māori people seeking pounamu (greenstone) from West Coast rivers. This was also a busy route during the 1860s, used by European explorers, gold prospectors, then runholders driving sheep to the West Coast. In the north of the park this tramp follows the wide, open Taramakau River, on the western side of the Main Divide, and crosses the low-level Harper Pass into the Hurunui Valley and neighbouring Lake Sumner Forest Park, eventually reaching the Lewis Pass highway. The ends of this tramp are some 350 km apart by road, but public transport is available. Travel is easy

on the broad flats of the Taramakau River, though high river levels of the main river and its tributaries can halt progress. There are several park huts.

Mountaineering

There are 16 mountains over 2000 m in the park. Many of these, in particular Mt Rolleston (2275 m), Mt Murchison (2408 m) and Mt Franklin (2145 m), are popular challenges for experienced climbers. Major routes are from Rome Ridge to Mt Rolleston, Philistine and Otirā Face to Mt Rolleston and Mt Murchison (the highest peak in the park) from Barker Hut. Avalanches are a constant threat. Mt Rolleston is relatively close to the main highway and offers challenging face climbs and ice routes during winter. Buttresses on Mt Temple also offer good winter ice climbing and summer rock climbing.

For climbing novices, the straightforward summer walks to Avalanche Peak and Mt Bealey are convenient spots to learn the skills of ice axe, crampon and rope use when snow-covered in winter. The New Zealand Alpine Club publishes a guide to climbing routes in the Arthur's Pass region.

Rock climbing

Outside the park but nearby there are bouldering opportunities on the world-renowned limestone outcrops at Castle Hill, 50 km from the park on the way to Christchurch.

Skiing

Skiing is a traditional pursuit in the park and surrounding mountains, particularly with Christchurch enthusiasts who for years have been able to travel here easily by road or rail. There are several ski fields in the region. Temple Basin is in the park, while there are two fields in neighbouring Craigieburn Forest Park and a further three in nearby ranges. For those with suitable experience there are ski-touring opportunities in the park. Some locations are Otirā Slide, Crow Glacier, Avalanche Peak basin and the Kelly Range.

Fishing
The Waimakariri, Poulter and Hawdon are among the more popular trout-fishing rivers in the park. Fishing licences are available from www.fishandgame.org.nz.

Hunting
Recreational hunting for red deer and chamois is encouraged. Popular areas are the upper Poulter Valley and Deception Valley. Hunting permits are available from the Department of Conservation office at 133 Victoria St, Christchurch – not at the Arthur's Pass Visitor Centre.

Alpine highway
State Highway 73, the highway that bisects the park, crosses the highest alpine pass of any road in the Southern Alps/Kā Tiritiri o te Moana. One of the features that unfolds from the highway as it climbs then descends from Arthur's Pass is the distinctive vegetation transitions of the park, all within an hour's driving. Tall beech forest in the lower, drier eastern valleys becomes stunted as the road gains altitude, then the trees give way to subalpine shrublands and tussock-filled valleys that are flanked by towering mountain walls. In the course of the descent to the West Coast rainforest, the trees grow tall again and podocarps, southern rātā and kāmahi emerge from the understorey trees, shrubs and ferns.

Top tips

- If visiting between November and February, be sure to look for the alpine flowers on the Dobson Nature Walk.
- Don't miss the Devils Punchbowl Falls.
- Climb to Avalanche Peak. It's the top summer day walk, with the best views of the park – weather permitting.
- Pause for photo stops looking up the Waimakariri Valley just after entering the park on SH73 (western side of the Bealey Bridge), looking up the Otirā headwaters towards Mt Rolleston, and at the scenic lookout at the Otirā Viaduct.
- Camp at Kellys Creek. It has a delightful creek for kids to play in and is especially brilliant in a good rātā flowering year.
- Walk the Mingha–Deception Valleys.
- Come in summer or winter – spring and autumn tend to be the wettest and windiest seasons.
- Take a walk around Arthur's Pass village and view the photographs at historic sites that show how it was in the early 20th century. Call at Jack's Hut (3 km towards the pass from the village) and see where this early roadman lived.
- Spend a night in Arthur's Pass village and listen for the calls of great spotted kiwi, roroa.

If the scenery from your vehicle isn't sufficiently awe-inspiring, many of the park's short walks, signposted along the highway, lead to waterfalls, alpine meadows and riverside picnic areas. An amazing engineering feature in the park is the Otirā Viaduct, completed in 1999 to protect the road from the huge shingle slides that occur across the Alpine Fault, which traverses the Otirā Gorge.

As it passes through the park, in particular between Arthur's Pass summit and Otirā, the road is steep and winding. It can be slippery with ice in winter and is sometimes closed by snow. Fuel is available in Arthur's Pass village, but the next fuel stops are at Kūmara, 59 km away on the West Coast and Springfield, 88 km from the village on the eastern side of the park.

An alternative to driving across Arthur's Pass is to take the Tranz Alpine train journey, which travels daily from Christchurch to Greymouth.

Information

Getting there: By road, SH73, 153 km from Christchurch and 98 km from Greymouth. By bus or train, daily services run between Christchurch and the West Coast.

When to go: Summer for tramping, scenery, alpine flowers. Winter for skiing, mountaineering.

Climate: Temperatures range from high twenties Celsius in summer to below freezing in winter. Heavy rainfall on the western side of the park, a drier climate in the east (up to 7000 mm per year in the west compared with 1500 mm in the east). Heavy snowfalls likely in winter. Sudden weather changes likely at any time of the year.

Accommodation and facilities: Accommodation in Arthur's Pass village includes backpacker and YHA hostels, bed-and-breakfast, motel and park campsite. Luxury lodge and hotel accommodation is available in nearby towns and high-country stations. In Arthur's Pass village there is a bar, restaurant, café and a few shops selling crafts, basic groceries and petrol. There is no bank or ATM. There are also no medical services, so take care on the road and in the hills. There are self-registration campsites at Kellys Creek and Klondyke Corner.

Commercial ventures: Local companies, some based in Christchurch, provide guided climbing, tramping and natural history tours. Ski and snowboarding equipment is available for hire at ski fields.

Further reading: Arthur's Pass Parkmap; NZMS 260 series topographical maps K33, L33; park brochures; *The Great Alpine Highway*, Christchurch and Canterbury Marketing; *Arthur's Pass: A Guide for Mountaineers*,

Graeme Kates (New Zealand Alpine Club); *Arthur's Pass Route Guide* series, Department of Conservation.

Special conditions: Mountain weather can change quickly. Wherever you go, even on a short walk and especially if heading above the bushline, take warm clothing and wet-weather gear.

Trampers should be aware that few rivers are bridged, so expect wet feet and be prepared for delays. It's safer to wait a day or so than risk crossing a flooded river. Before your trip, check the forecast and leave your intentions at the visitor centre. Do remember to sign out – searches are expensive. Some huts (Carrington, Hawdon, Edwards, Casey and Goat Pass) have radios that can be used to contact staff during opening hours at the Arthur's Pass National Park Visitor Centre.

In winter, routes will be harder to find and there can be serious avalanche danger in many areas. The website www.softrock.co.nz provides information on snow conditions and avalanche hazards in the Arthur's Pass region. Unless you have appropriate levels of skills and fitness, stay away from avalanche-prone tracks and routes.

Kea are bold, curious birds. Please don't encourage them by feeding them, and take care not to let them damage your possessions – boots, packs, car tyres, windscreen wipers, for example – as they have a tendency to do when bored or hungry.

Visitor centre: The Arthur's Pass National Park Visitor Centre in the middle of Arthur's Pass village provides information, weather forecasts, hut tickets, maps, brochures and hunting permits plus displays and an audiovisual about the park. There is also a small retail shop with basic tramping gear, clothing and conservation-related products.

Arthur's Pass National Park Visitor Centre
SH73
PO Box 8
Arthur's Pass village
Phone 0-3-318 9211
Email arthurspassvc@doc.govt.nz
Open daily (except Christmas Day) 8 am to 5 pm (summer);
8.30 am to 4.30 pm (winter)

Aoraki/Mt Cook National Park

Location: Southern Alps/Kā Tiritiri o te Moana, central South Island

Features: New Zealand's highest mountain ■ longest glacier ■ mass of mountain peaks over 3000 m high ■ glacial lakes ■ mountain tarns and glacier-gouged valleys ■ World Heritage Area

Activities: short walks ■ tramping ■ mountaineering ■ glacier skiing ■ ski-mountaineering ■ ski-touring ■ heli-skiing ■ scenic flights and glacier landings ■ glacier lake cruises

This is a true alpine park, a World Heritage Area that has within its boundaries the country's highest mountains, longest glaciers and most permanent snow and ice fields. Part of the Te Wāhipounamu – South West New Zealand World Heritage Area, Aoraki/Mt Cook has a long tradition of tourism and today remains an extremely popular park. Dedicated climbers tackle the challenges of the premier mountaineering region in all of New Zealand and Australia, while more sedentary visitors arrive by coach or plane to marvel at the grandeur of the terrain.

Between these two extremes, more visitors explore the walking and tramping tracks, admiring alpine tarns and flowers and mountain and glacier panoramas. Whether walking, climbing, ski-touring or sipping a coffee in the Aoraki/Mt Cook village, simply being in the park – dwarfed by mountains, with the not uncommon roar of avalanches crashing into distant valleys – is an awe-inspiring experience.

About the park

Aoraki/Mt Cook lies on the eastern side of the Southern Alps/Kā Tiritiri o te Moana and is bordered along its main dividing ridge by Westland/ Tai Poutini National Park.

The park is named for its highest mountain, Aoraki/Mt Cook. The Maˉori people of the South Island, Ngāi Tahu, regard Aoraki as a god. In Ngāi Tahu mythology Aoraki was the son of the sky father Raki (also known as Rangi), and the South Island his capsized canoe. When the canoe turned over, Aoraki and his crew climbed to the high side and became the great mountains of the Southern Alps/Kā Tiritiri o te Moana. This special relationship between the mountains and Ngāi Tahu was officially

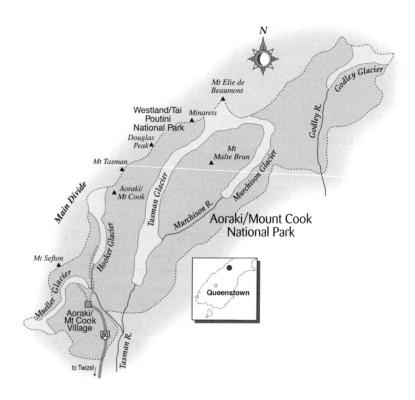

acknowledged in 1997, when the park was given the dual name of Aoraki/Mt Cook. The name Cook comes from James Cook, the first English explorer to visit New Zealand.

Aoraki/Mt Cook (3754 m) is surrounded by more than 20 mountain peaks that are over 3000 m. These mountains have been pushed upwards by two of the earth's tectonic plates as they collide along the South Island Alpine Fault. However, this powerful mountain-building process has been countered by constant erosion, as the sedimentary greywackes and argillites that make up the mountains have been worn down by the mighty forces of water, wind and ice. This process continues today.

The challenge of climbing these mountains has been a tradition in the park since the 1880s. Aoraki/Mt Cook was first climbed in 1894 and the European concept of mountain guiding that developed in the park in those pioneering times is now well established. Climbing Aoraki/Mt Cook will always be the premier challenge but neighbouring mountains – Tasman, Sefton, Malte Brun, La Perouse and Elie de Beaumont – are also formidable climbs. The park has proved to be a fine training ground for some of New Zealand's great Himalayan climbers, including Sir Edmund Hillary and the late Rob Hall and Gary Ball. Several high-altitude huts and bivouacs, some perched on precarious mountainside sites, provide shelter for mountaineers from the sudden and severe storms that frequently lash this formidable environment.

Glaciers

Glaciation is a compelling feature of the park's landscape. Over one-third of the 70,000 ha park is covered with glacial ice as five major and many smaller glaciers slowly gouge the valley floors, transporting huge loads of rubble from the mountains and depositing them at the glacier terminals in piles called moraines. As the ice gradually melts, milky coloured lakes filled with ground rubble and lined with glacial rock flour form at the glacier terminals.

The constantly changing landscapes these glaciers create are both a pleasure and problem for park visitors. Boat trips across the glacial lakes to the terminals provide a fascinating option for less energetically inclined tourists, but the growing moraine walls cause difficulties for climbers seeking access to the park's upper valleys.

Today's glaciers are but tiny remnants of the immense glaciers that 40,000 years ago extended well beyond the park and carved the huge basins of lakes Tekapō, Pūkaki and Ohau. Nevertheless, at 29 km in length, Tasman Glacier is one of the longest glaciers in the temperate regions of the world. While it slowly but powerfully continues its natural landscaping work, the Tasman also presents a range of sightseeing and glacier-skiing options for park visitors.

Life in the mountains

The ice, snow and rock of the mountains and glaciers might seem an inhospitable environment, yet the grasslands, alpine shrublands, tussockfields, rock gardens, scree slopes and beech forest are home to a great range of plant life, including several species endemic to the park. Most notable are the alpine flowers, in particular the mountain buttercup *Ranunculus lyalli*, commonly misnamed the Mt Cook lily and almost as symbolic of the park as the mountain itself.

Top tips

- Wander into the Hooker Valley. Enjoy the summer flowers, glacial lake and mountain grandeur, and share the inquisitive company of a kea. Take time to reflect at the Alpine Memorial, remembering those who have died in these mountains.
- Take a cruise on a glacier lake. Touch an iceberg. Confront the melting ice face of New Zealand's longest glacier.
- If fit and able, and weather conditions are favourable, take on the 4 hour (one way) climb to Mueller Hut.

Several native birds species survive in the harsh alpine environment, including rock wrens, pipits, New Zealand falcons and kea.

An integral part of Aoraki/Mt Cook history and tradition centres on the Hermitage tourist hotel. The present hotel, located in Aoraki/Mt Cook village, is the third in this area. Flood and fire destroyed its predecessors which, since 1884, have accommodated climbers and tourists from all around the world who have journeyed to experience the splendour of these mountains.

What to do

Short walks

While technical mountaineering expertise is a requirement to climb the high peaks and passes of the park, less adventurous visitors can explore a surprising range of alpine environments, walking on top-quality trails, only an hour or so from the park village.

Hooker Valley (Aoraki/Mt Cook village) 2 to 4 hours return

One of the park's most popular walks, featuring views of Aoraki/ Mt Cook, and the glacier-gouged Hooker Valley and its creamy-coloured river and glacier terminal lake. The walk crosses two sturdy swingbridges (turning around at the second reduces the walk to 2 hours) then heads up the valley towards Aoraki/Mt Cook. In early summer the mountain buttercup should be easily found. A short but worthy side trip is to the Alpine Memorial, a fine viewpoint and contemplative spot, as it remembers those who have died in climbing tragedies in the park.

Kea Point (Aoraki/Mt Cook village) 2 hours return

A gentle wander through subalpine grasslands and shrubs to the Mueller Glacier moraine wall, and a stunning viewpoint that encompasses the big mountains Aoraki/Mt Cook, Sefton and Footstool, plus Mueller Glacier Lake and Hooker Valley. The walk can be reduced to 1 hour by starting from the White Horse Hill campsite. Springtime sees avalanches thundering off Mt Sefton, a safe distance across Mueller Valley.

Red Tarns (Aoraki/Mt Cook village) 2 hours return

A steep but magnificently rewarding climb behind the village, up very solidly built steps to two little red-coloured tarns nestled in a tussock basin on the lower slopes of Mt Sebastopol. As with all walks in the park, the mountain and glacier views are outstanding. Closer at hand, in summer, look for alpine flowers. (A more challenging, unmarked route climbs from the tarns and onto a steep scree ridge to the Sebastopol summit. Allow a further 4 hours return from the tarns, and pick a good day.)

Sealy Tarns (Aoraki/Mt Cook village) 3 to 4 hours return

Steeper and surely even more rewarding for the extra effort required, this track turns off the Kea Point walk and zigzags uphill to the Sealy Tarns, in a narrow mountainside terrace. There are stunning views of the surrounding peaks and Hooker Glacier and, in summer, an abundance of alpine flowers.

Blue Lakes and Tasman Glacier (Tasman Valley Road)
40 minutes return

In the Tasman Valley, the track meanders from Blue Lakes Shelter to the moraine wall and a viewpoint of the glacier and Blue Lakes. Now more green than blue, these lakes are a good (albeit refreshing) swimming spot in summer.

Tasman Glacier Lake (Tasman Valley Road) 1 hour return

Branching off the Blue Lakes walk, this track leads to a viewpoint of the glacier's terminal lake and source of the Tasman River. In summer look out for icebergs; in winter the lake freezes. On either side, rockfalls on the steep and unstable walls of lateral moraine are constant. It is a dramatic, harsh and desolate environment.

Longer walk

Mueller Hut (Aoraki/Mt Cook village) 3 to 4 hours one way

During winter, climbing experience and equipment is needed for this 1000 m climb, but from mid November to late March if conditions are favourable it is achievable by those with moderate tramping experience. Navigation is difficult in poor weather, with much of the route marked only by cairns and orange markers. Seek advice on snow and weather conditions before starting. With cautions thus heeded, this magic spot yields a 360-degree panorama of glaciers, ice cliffs, rock faces and New Zealand's highest peaks. The climb leads past Sealy Tarns through alpine shrubs, herbfields and scree slopes. If you are staying overnight, close to Mueller Hut a rock scramble/climb of the 1933 m Mt Olivier is feasible. Beyond that, the terrain is suitable only for mountaineers.

Alpine passes

Ball Pass 2 to 3 days

This unmarked crossing of the Aoraki/Mt Cook Range, between the Hooker and Tasman Valleys, includes steep alpine terrain, snow, scree and rocky bluffs. The best season is December to March – snow limits travel at other times, though difficult conditions, rockfalls and avalanches can occur throughout the year. If travelling with a guide, the crossing is feasible for fit, experienced hikers with good balance. Otherwise, mountaineering experience is essential. Caroline Hut, on the Ball Pass route, is owned by a private guiding company.

Copland Pass 3 days

A classic but currently questionable alpine route, crossing from Hooker Valley, over Copland Pass and into Westland/Tai Poutini National Park on the western side of the Main Divide. In the Copland Valley, West Coast forests and natural hot pools are appealing features.

However, erosion in the Hooker Valley has rendered the traditional approach route inaccessible. Alternative routes are constantly changing and often very dangerous. Most guiding companies take the eastern side of Hooker Valley, then cross the Hooker Glacier to rejoin the traditional route. Whatever the approach, Copland Pass itself is extremely steep, and not for the faint-hearted. Trampers must have alpine route experience, and guides are highly recommended. Anyone considering this route should check current conditions at the visitor centre.

Mountaineering

The mountains of the park offer world-class climbing, with 20 peaks over 3000 m and some 150 named summits over 2000 m. Although not high by international standards, the mountains have many long and difficult routes that call for ability to handle snow, rock and ice in one climb.

There are more challenges. Storms can arrive unexpectedly and last for days or weeks. Winds can be fierce. Snow conditions can be poor for long periods. The entire region is prone to avalanche danger and there are a number of active ice cliffs. The traditional climbing season extends from November to March, but glacier travel can become difficult in summer as crevasse bridges melt and collapse.

Nevertheless, the high mountains draw climbers from around the world. Professional climbing guides operate throughout the park, leading guided ascents and beginner and advanced climbing courses.

The Grand Plateau, in the Tasman Valley, is the main approach for climbs on New Zealand's two highest mountains, Aoraki/Mt Cook and Mt Tasman. Ngāi Tahu tradition encourages climbers not to stand on the very top of Aoraki/Mt Cook. More difficult approaches to the western flanks of Aoraki/Mt Cook and Mt Hicks lead from the upper Hooker Valley. Several rock and snow peaks lie at the head of the Tasman Glacier. To the east, the Malte Brun Range offers a range of shorter climbs, from simple snow and ice ridges to challenging faces. Further afield, the Murchison and Godley valleys offer more remote climbing experiences. In contrast, the Sealy Range is one of the park's most accessible areas and is regarded as a good training ground and introduction to the region.

Rock climbing

There are limited opportunities within the boundaries of the park. There is some bouldering around the White Horse Hill campsite, and the bluffs on Mt Sebastopol offer a number of sport and traditional climbing routes for those with equipment and experience. There is extremely good multi-pitch traditional climbing at Twin Stream, just south of the park. Access is via a walk of several hours or by helicopter; climbers must get permission from Glentanner Station.

Skiing

Skiing in the park takes a variety of forms, mostly guided. In winter glacier skiing is popular, flying onto the Tasman Glacier by ski-plane and skiing (intermediate grade) back for up to 20 km through ice caves and amazing scenery. The glacier is not steep enough for snowboards.

Heli-skiing is also a winter activity, for advanced skiers and boarders on steeper glaciers and other slopes.

In winter Mueller Hut is a base for ski-touring on the Sealy Range. There is considerable avalanche danger on the access route during winter and spring – check conditions with park staff before setting out.

Ski-mountaineering, using skis to access climbs or to descend, is another option in the park.

Glacier lakes

Melt lakes have formed at the terminal snouts of the glaciers. On the Mueller, Hooker and Tasman Glaciers this melting process has, over the past 15 to 20 years, formed lakes big enough to launch boats and kayaks. Today motorboat cruises on the murky, milky-coloured glacial waters, amid drifting icebergs, on the Tasman Glacier lake and kayak trips on the Mueller Glacier lake provide a rather different perspective of the park.

Scenic flights

Somewhat incongruous, in this immense, natural world of rock and ice and natural elements, is the steady drone of aircraft engines. Scenic flights and glacier landings, by ski-planes and helicopters, and access flights for climbers and skiers are a major aspect of tourism in the park. Flights depart from airfields at the village, Glentanner and Tekapō.

Hunting

Introduced thar and chamois live in the high alpine habitats of the park. Hunting is permitted throughout the year. Permits must be obtained from the Department of Conservation. Hunters must also sign their intentions at the visitor centre when entering the park.

Information

Getting there: By road via SH8 from Timaru to Lake Pūkaki, then SH80 to Aoraki/Mt Cook village. Travel time is about 3 hours from Timaru, and about 4 hours from Christchurch. By bus, several coach tours include Aoraki/Mt Cook on their tourist itineraries. A shuttle bus also connects with InterCity services at Twizel, 70 km from Aoraki/Mt Cook village.

When to go: For sightseeing visitors, any time. The mountains are spectacular year-round, though spring and summer are best for alpine flowers. For mountaineering, spring and summer (November to March) are the preferred months, depending on snow and ice conditions. Winter and spring are best for glacier skiing and ski-touring, though there is avalanche danger.

Climate: Subject to sudden and dramatic change, with heavy rainfall, snow and gale-force nor'wester winds occurring at any time of the year. There are also long settled periods of fine weather and it can be very hot in summer, up to 32°C, and ultraviolet rays can be intense. In winter, frosts and snow are likely at low levels.

Accommodation and facilities: At Aoraki/Mt Cook village there is a range of accommodation, from the historic Hermitage four-star hotel to motels, YHA hostel, Aoraki Lodge and the park's White Horse Hill campsite. There is also a bar, souvenir shop, park visitor centre shop, restaurants, self-serve petrol and an alpine guide shop, where specialist climbing and ski equipment is available for hire. A limited amount of groceries can be purchased at the Hermitage coffee shop.

Further accommodation (cabins, campervan/camping and back-packers) is available at Glentanner Park, 15 minutes' drive from the village.

There are 18 park huts, ranging from small bivouacs with minimal facilities to large, well-equipped huts with solar lighting, water, gas, radio and toilet. A daily radio schedule to mountain huts is operated by park staff, providing a weather forecast and checking that parties are safe. Caroline Hut, on the Ball Pass route, is privately owned.

Commercial ventures: Guided climbing, tramping and walking, climbing courses, ski-plane and helicopter scenic flights and glacier landings, glacier skiing, heli-skiing, glacier lake boat and kayak cruises, 4WD tours of Tasman Valley.

Further reading: Aoraki/Mt Cook/Westland/Tai Poutini Parkmap; NZMS 260 series topographical maps H36, H37, I36, I35; *Aoraki Mt Cook: A Guide for Mountaineers*, Alex Palman (New Zealand Alpine Club).

Special conditions: These mountains, and the unpredictable, at times fearsome weather they attract, should not be underestimated. Park staff undertake an average of 30 searches every year, and rescue people from anywhere from the top of Aoraki/Mt Cook to the end of a 1 hour walking track. Each year several people die in the park. Most have been climbers, but increasing numbers have perished on tramping trips. It is particularly important that all those leaving for a trip in the park seek good advice, are properly equipped, have suitable experience or hire a guide, and fill in an intentions form at the park's visitor centre before leaving, then sign out when they return.

Visitor centre: The park visitor centre in Aoraki/Mt Cook village has interpretive displays and sells books, maps, hut tickets and souvenirs. Information, advice and current weather, avalanche, snow and track conditions are also available, as is the trip intentions book for anyone planning a trip in the park.

Aoraki/Mt Cook Visitor Centre
PO Box 5
Mt Cook 8770
Phone 0-3-405 1186
Email mtcookvc@doc.govt.nz
Open daily 8.30 am to 6 pm (summer) or 5 pm (winter)

Westland/Tai Poutini National Park

Location: South Island West Coast

Features: World Heritage Area ■ world's most accessible glaciers ■ some of New Zealand's highest mountains ■ rainforest ■ rivers ■ lakes ■ lagoons ■ wildlife

Activities: short walks ■ glacier walks ■ wildlife watching ■ tramping ■ climbing (experienced climbers only) ■ kayaking ■ nature tours ■ scenic drives ■ scenic flights

There are few places in the world where natural wilderness remains intact from mountaintops through to the sea, and where glaciers meet with rainforest. Westland/Tai Poutini is a park of superlatives, and one of four neighbouring parks which make up the 2,600,000 ha of Te Wāhipounamu – South West New Zealand World Heritage Area.

Westland/Tai Poutini has within its boundaries some of New Zealand's highest mountains and fastest-moving glaciers, as well as permanent snowfields, temperate rainforests, rivers, lakes, lagoons and coastline. The mountains rise abruptly from the coastal lowlands. Within a mere 20 km, from its shared boundary with Aoraki/Mt Cook National Park on the South Island's Main Divide, the park plunges from over 3000 m in altitude to sea level.

The park's two major glaciers, Fox Glacier/Te Moeka o Tuawe and Franz Josef Glacier/Kā Roimata o Hine Hukatere, attract thousands of visitors every year. Aside from glacier walks (which include guided options), there are many other short walks in the park that explore some natural heritage or stunning outlook, mountain reflections, primeval rainforest, glacial lakes, rugged coastline and a lagoon teeming with wildlife. Walking to or boating in Ōkārito Lagoon, adjacent to the park, is a birdwatcher's dream. There is one major tramping route in the park and several challenging mountaineering routes.

About the park

The Southern Alps/Kā Tiritiri o te Moana have been thrust upwards by collision of the earth's crustal plates along the Alpine Fault. In Westland that uplift has occurred rapidly (in a geological sense), hence the dramatically steep rise of the mountains from the lowland plains.

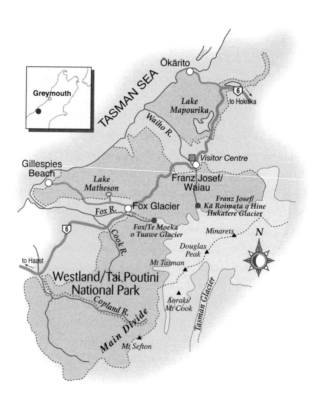

The biggest peaks, all over 3000 m, are Tasman, Douglas, Sefton, Elie de Beaumont and the Minarets. These are popular mountaineering challenges, though stormy weather, impassable river gorges and vast snowfields with hidden crevasses make climbing from the west side of the Alps a difficult proposition. New Zealand's highest mountain, Aoraki/Mt Cook, stands beyond the park boundary but is nevertheless prominent on the Westland skyline.

Countering the ongoing uplift process have been the eroding forces of ice, water and wind. Westland receives one of the heaviest rainfalls in the world. The mountains stand in the path of prevailing moist westerly winds, which sweep across the Tasman Sea and cool rapidly as they are forced upwards against the bulk of the mountain chain. Heavy rain at the coast turns to huge snowfalls at higher altitudes, and land above 2500 m is covered with permanent snow. These snowfields accumulate in large basins, or névés, and as the weight of new snow forces air from underlying snow, compressed snow crystals turn to blue glacial ice. Gravity forces the glacial ice downhill, and so the glaciers begin their powerful journey.

Glaciers

There are more than 60 glaciers in Westland/Tai Poutini – more than 60 rivers of ice that scour their way down the park's valleys, breaking into a jumble of crevasses and grinding bedrock to powder as they move, and eventually melting in the warmer temperatures of lower altitudes.

Two glaciers are dominating features of the park. Franz Josef Glacier/Kā Roimata o Hine Hukatere and Fox Glacier/Te Moeka o Tuawe are among the most accessible glaciers in the world, and are the only low-altitude glaciers to exist at such temperate latitudes. They attract thousands of tourists each year.

The two glaciers are fed from particularly huge snowfields, which cram into steep and narrow valleys. Hence they move exceptionally fast and reach unusually low altitudes. They have been known to move 3 to 4 m each day (by comparison, the Tasman Glacier in Aoraki/Mt Cook

National Park moves at 650 mm a day). Their retreating paths have played a major hand in shaping the park landscape, with a legacy of lakes, moraines and glacial deposits.

Rainforests

Dense rainforests that extend across the lowlands from the glaciers to the sea thrive in mild temperatures and heavy rainfall. Glacial moraines and old river terraces are covered with majestic rimu; the Ōkārito and Waikukupa forests support the highest densities of rimu forest in the country. New Zealand's tallest tree, kahikatea, dominates the wetter alluvial plains and lake margins. Within these forests flourish smaller trees, shrubs, vines, ferns, mosses and epiphytes. While the podocarps flourish, the park is distinctive for its lack of beech forest. Beech is dominant in many South Island national parks but is absent in Westland.

The lower mountain slopes and valleys are filled with southern rātā and kāmahi. Close to the glacier terminals, tiny but hardy lichens and mosses begin the slow process of plant colonisation and provide visual contrast in the stark landscape of ice and rock.

Wildlife diversity

Many of New Zealand's native bird species, including seasonal migrants, are present in the park, along with a significant array of lizards, snails, bats and aquatic fauna.

The lowland rainforests are laced with lakes, lagoons and deep, slow-flowing waterways that provide natural habits unrivalled in New Zealand. These places support 17 species of native freshwater fish, plus many species of waterfowl, including one of New Zealand's rarest water birds, the southern crested grebe.

Kahikatea-fringed coastal lagoons, which occupy troughs of former glacial tongues, are peaceful refuges compared with the bouldery beaches of the park, constantly hammered by westerly ocean swells. Just outside the northern margins of the park is Ōkārito Lagoon, the largest remaining natural estuary in New Zealand and a birdwatcher's paradise. This lagoon supports thousands of native and migratory birds and is the main feeding ground of royal spoonbills and white herons. The white herons breed nearby in the kahikatea trees beside the Waitangoroto River at the same time of year as the annual migration in the river of galaxiid, their favoured food.

The park's Ōkārito Forest is home to a small endemic population of rowi (Ōkārito brown kiwi). These birds number approximately 200 and conservation staff are carrying out research and management work to ensure their long-term survival.

Park visitors are likely to come across kea when they visit the glaciers, or hear the raucous screech of kākā, the kea's bush parrot relative, high above the trees while on a lowland forest walk. They are less likely to spot the tiny but hardy rock wren, which lives high above the treeline, or the blue duck, which frequents remote mountain streams. Long-tailed bats, Westland skinks and carnivorous land snails are even harder to find.

People in the park

Westland/Tai Poutini has never been a heavily populated region. Early Māori lived in a few coastal settlements and passed through in search of pounamu (greenstone). Nevertheless the glaciers and their surrounding mountains and lakes have a special place in Māori lore.

Hine Hukatere, an adventurous maiden who loved mountaineering above all other pastimes, frequently persuaded her lover, Tuawe, to accompany her on escapades into the hills. On one such expedition the unfortunate Tuawe, who had never been as fond of climbing as his sweetheart, slipped on the snowy mountain slopes and plunged to his death. Hine's tears were frozen by the gods as a memorial to her grief – frozen in the glacier Kā Roimata o Hine Hukatere, meaning 'tears of the avalanche girl'. Fox Glacier is named Te Moeka o Tuawe, 'the resting place of Tuawe'.

Sealers stayed briefly to exploit the coast's fur seal populations and, in the 1860s, the discovery of gold brought a short-lived boom, followed by a bust. Some of the park's short walks lead to historic features relating to this mining era. There has been some farm development on the lowlands near the park. The glaciers, lakes and rainforest have long been tourist attractions, and from the early 20th century guiding and accommodation services have been established to cater for the growing numbers of visitors. Tourism is now the economic mainstay of the region: a host of accommodation, guiding, kayaking and scenic flight services operate from Franz Josef/Waiau and Fox Glacier villages.

Natural wilderness continues well beyond the southern park boundary, much of it protected as scenic reserve. There can be few places in the world where one can drive for hours on a main highway through rainforest with snow-covered mountains on one side and remote surf beaches on the other, or kayak a gently flowing river from the base of a glacier, through rainforest, to the sea.

What to do

Short walks

Following is a selection of the best of many outstanding short walks available in Westland/Tai Poutini. Park brochures offer more ideas, and give clear access details for all of these walks.

Fox Glacier/Te Moeka o Tuawe Valley Walk (Fox Glacier)
30 minutes one way
A riverbed walk to a close-up look of the glacier terminal face. The track crosses several small creeks, then climbs around huge boulders to get close to the glacier. Note that ice movement and erosion make this region highly changeable, and walkers should take note of warning signs and barriers.

Chalet Lookout Track (Fox Glacier) 1.5 hours return

This was the main approach route used by glacier guides before the glacier retreated. Today the same route leads to an excellent viewpoint. In the late 19th and early 20th century the glacier extended far beyond its present terminal, and this walk passes several moraines, boulders and deposits left behind by the retreating ice. It also climbs gently through southern rātā and kāmahi forest, so keep an eye and ear out for native birds such as tūī, bellbirds and fantails. Note that this track crosses several streams that can quickly become dangerous in heavy rain.

Fox Glacier/Te Moeka o Tuawe River Walk (Fox Glacier)
30 minutes return

A link between the north and south glacier access roads that leads to a glacier viewpoint and passes through different stages of forest growth related to the glacier's retreat. The track crosses the Fox River by a 70 m suspension bridge. Today's walkers will be surprised to learn that the glacier could be seen from this bridge as recently as 1970. The track then passes through young kāmahi and hardwood forest on a glacial surface that was covered by ice a hundred years ago, then climbs onto an older terrace covered by more mature southern rātā and kāmahi forest. Over a long period of time the natural forest succession here will result in the establishment of tall podocarp trees, such as rimu and tōtara.

Moraine Walk (Fox Glacier) 40 minutes return

A wander across old glacial moraines through a prime example of luxuriant South Westland rainforest, which shows clearly how quickly plants colonise after the ice has retreated. The varying ages of the vegetation here reflect the different ages of the glacial moraines on which it is growing.

Minnehaha Track (Fox Glacier village) 30 minutes return

A delightful streamside walk in lush West Coast rainforest. With glistening mosses, lichens and ferns, it is good in any weather. The path is suitable for wheelchairs.

Lake Matheson Walk (west of Fox Glacier village) 1.5 hours loop

One of the most popular walks in the park, leading to a classic mountain reflection scene that's often shown on calendars and postcards. Lake Matheson was formed when the retreating Fox Glacier/Te Moeka o Tuawe ground a depression that later filled with water. Today the lake is surrounded by tall kahikatea and rimu forest, the brown colour of its water a result of organic matter leached from the forest floor. The walk is well defined and gently graded, and suitable for people of medium to low fitness. There are two excellent viewpoints from where, when conditions are calm and clear, New Zealand's highest mountains – Aoraki/Mt Cook and Tasman – will be reflected in the forest-framed lake. Film manufacturers no doubt made fortunes here before the advent of digital photography.

Galway Beach Walk (Gillespies Beach) 3.5 hours return

A wild, primeval piece of coastline, with a forest-fringed lagoon, mining history and great mountain views. The discovery that the black sands along this coastline were gold-rich led to a busy but brief period of mining activity and a small town sprang up at Gillespies Beach during the 1890s. A miners' cemetery near the car park is a reminder of the harsh environment the miners lived and worked in. A 15-minute walk leads across scrub-covered gold tailings to the remains of a gold dredge, used briefly in the 1930s, and it is another 30 minutes along the beach to Gillespies Lagoon. Footbridges lead over the lagoon, then the track follows an old miner's pack track to a sturdy tunnel built in the 1870s to provide high-tide access along the coast, which leads to a magnificent viewpoint overlooking the beach. Just before the tunnel a track branches right and leads through tall rimu forest to the fur seal colony at Galway Beach.

Franz Josef Glacier/Kā Roimata o Hine Hukatere Walk (Franz Josef Glacier) 1.5 hours return

A walk along the riverbed to the terminal face of the glacier. This is a highly volatile environment subject to heavy rain, flooding rivers and changing river channels and, at the glacier's terminal face, ice collapse and rockfall. Barriers and warning signs should be heeded, and climbing onto the glacier should only be attempted with a guided tour.

Sentinel Rock (Franz Josef Glacier) 20 minutes return

A steady climb onto a huge schist boulder that withstood ice action and emerged in the 1860s as the glacier retreated. It is now colonised by *Olearia* shrubs and young kāmahi and southern rātā forest, and provides a lookout point for grand views of the glacier and Waiho Valley.

Top tips

- Take a close look at a couple of the world's fastest-moving glaciers – the Fox/Te Moeka o Tuawe and the Franz Josef /Ka Roimata o Hine Hukatere – on the Chalet Lookout Track and the Sentinel Rock Walk respectively.
- Catch the classic mountain reflection photo by visiting Lake Matheson in the early morning or evening, when the mountains are more likely to be clearly visible and the lake surface unruffled.
- Drive to Peak View Point, 10 km from Fox Glacier village, for a panoramic view of Aoraki/Mt Cook, Mt Tasman, Fox Glacier/Te Moeka o Tuawe and the grand expanse of the Southern Alps/ Kā Titiri o te Moana.
- If the weather is wet, enjoy Minnehaha Walk as it meanders beside the bubbling Minnehaha Stream through rainforest that in fact needs the rain to exist. At night, take a torch and spot the glow worms.
- Drive to Gillespies Beach, a classic, wild West Coast beach with dumping surf, piled driftwood and salt-laden sea mists. Think of the miners who once tried to eke a living here. It is outside but close to the park.
- Explore nearby Ōkārito Lagoon, one of New Zealand's outstanding bird habitats, by foot, kayak or guided tour.

Douglas Walk (Franz Josef Glacier) 1 hour loop

A loop track over glacial moraines through a succession of vegetation types, each representing a different stage of regrowth behind retreating ice and/or different soil types. Features include Peter's Pool, a reflective kettle lake and the historic Douglas suspension bridge.

Longer walk

Mt Fox (SH 6 south of Fox Glacier village) 8 hours return

A steep climb with limited track formation through dense bush to Mt Fox (1021 m). Beware of sudden weather changes. The route begins in lowland rimu rainforest and changes to montane kāmahi/rātā forest then subalpine mountain cedar as altitude is gained. From Mt Fox (a great viewpoint) the route continues through snow tussock grasslands and alpine herbfields to a second high point at 1345 m. Start early in the morning so as to be on the mountaintop before cloud covers the view of the glaciers, coastline and the Southern Alps/Kā Tiritiri o te Moana.

Multi-day tramping trip

Welcome Flat 2 days return

A popular trip up the Copland River valley through dense rainforest to natural hot pools and a hut at Welcome Flat. It is part of an alpine crossing that climbs onto the Main Divide via the Copland Pass, then descends into the Hooker Valley, a route suitable only for experienced climbers with ice-climbing equipment. Most trampers simply walk the 17 km to Welcome Flat and return to the West Coast. Welcome Flat Hut accommodates up to 31 people on a first-come, first-served basis, though given its increasing popularity it is expected a booking system will soon be in place. The track follows the valley floor and crosses several small creeks that are prone to flooding during heavy rain.

Ōkārito Lagoon

Next to the park is one of New Zealand's premier birdwatching locations. Surrounded by rainforests, overlooked by the Southern Alps/Kā Tiritiri o te Moana and encompassing the slow-moving Ōkārito River and its ever-changing tidal delta, Ōkārito's 5000 ha of shallow waterways and wetlands provide a habitat for thousands of native birds. More than 72 bird species have been recorded, including royal spoonbills, fernbirds, bitterns, little shags, migratory waders and all of New Zealand's mainland species. Special residents include the only population of rowi (Ōkārito brown kiwi), and white herons.

There is a variety of ways to explore the lagoon: by foot, kayak or with a guided nature tour. There are three walking tracks. Pākiki Walk (30 minutes) climbs through kāmahi and rimu forest to a superb 360-degree lookout point, taking in the lagoon, coastline, mountains (including Aoraki/Mt Cook) and a glimpse of Franz Josef Glacier/Kā Roimata o Hine Hukatere. Ōkārito Trig (1.25 hours) leads to a second, equally breathtaking panorama. Three Mile Lagoon (2.75 hours) follows an old pack track south to a smaller, sheltered estuary fringed with impressive rimu forest. At low tide you can return via the beach – tide times are posted at the start of the walk.

The walks are stunning, but paddling quietly onto the lagoon itself in a kayak, into forest-lined channels where shags, herons and bush birds feed and roost, can be a very special experience. It is best to catch a high tide as you paddle in, and beware of being stranded on a tidal flat!

The white heron breeding sanctuary is in Waitangiroto Nature Reserve. Entry is by permit only, through White Heron Sanctuary Tours at Whataroa, which operates the only tours to view these birds in their nesting site. There is no access to the sanctuary from Ōkārito.

Mountaineering

There are several challenging climbs in Westland/Tai Poutini, in particular Tasman, Douglas, Sefton, Elie de Beaumont and the Minarets. (Although on the Main Divide, Aoraki/Mt Cook is generally climbed from the eastern side.) Climbing access from the West Coast side of the Alps is hampered by weather, river gorges and vast snowfields with hidden crevasses. However, professional guiding companies operate in the park, with many trips accessing the mountains by helicopter.

Fishing

Lake Mapourika is a popular spot for fishing of introduced trout and salmon. Fishing licences are available from service stations in Fox Glacier and Franz Josef/Waiau townships, and online at www. fishandgame.org.nz.

Hunting

Hunting for introduced thar and chamois is popular, in particular in the valleys of the Karangarua River and its tributaries. Introduced red deer are also present in the park. Hunting permits are available from Department of Conservation offices.

Information

Getting there: By road via SH6 (the Haast Highway), 135 km south of Hokitika. There are daily bus services. Nearest airport is Hokitika.
When to go: Any time.
Climate: Mild temperatures, heavy rainfall (5000 mm per year at Franz

A spectacular vantage point looking into West Mātukituki Valley from Cascade Saddle in Mt Aspiring National Park. The saddle links with Rees Valley, also a popular tramping valley, although bluffs and slippery snowgrass slopes make this a potentially treacherous alpine crossing. (DP)

Above: Routeburn River, Mt Aspiring National Park, near the eastern end of the Routeburn Track, a New Zealand Great Walk. (SB)

Left: Snow marguerites in the Olivine Wilderness Area, Mt Aspiring National Park. (DP)

Opposite top: Tramping off the beaten track in the Rock Burn Valley, Mt Aspiring National Park. (DP)

Opposite bottom: Mitre Peak, Milford Sound/Piopiotahi, Fiordland National Park, in typically sombre, misty mood. (SB)

Opposite top: Lake Marian, Fiordland. This classic, glacier-gouged mountain lake is just a few hours' walk from the Hollyford Valley. (DP)

Opposite bottom: Lake Mackenzie, on the Fiordland side of the Routeburn Track. (SB)

Right: Crossing the Clinton River on the Milford Track, New Zealand's most famous Great Walk. (DP)

Below: Dusky dolphins. The fiords and remote coastline of Fiordland support a rich and diverse marine life. (DH)

Opposite: East Ruggedy Beach, Rakiura National Park. Dunes, tenuously stabilised by sand-binding plants, dominate many of Rakiura's beaches. (SB)

Above: West Ruggedy, one of the wild beaches along Rakiura's North West Circuit, an 8 to 12 day tramping route. (DH)

Right: The yellow-eyed penguin, one of the world's rarest penguins, is occasionally seen in Rakiura National Park. (DH)

Left: Rimu forest stands tall above a thick carpet of crown ferns in Rakiura National Park. (DP)

Below: Mason Bay, on the western side of Rakiura, is becoming a popular tramping destination. (SB)

Josef, 10,000 mm per year further inland), heavy snowfalls in the mountains. Storms occur at any time of the year, but spring and early summer are particularly wet. Extended dry periods can occur during June and July.

Accommodation and facilities: Franz Josef/Waiau and Fox Glacier villages each have a shop, petrol sales, restaurants and a range of accommodation (hotels, motels, hostels and campgrounds). Accommodation should be booked in advance during summer months. There is a café at the Lake Matheson car park.

Commercial ventures: Glacier guides, alpine guides, scenic flights, lagoon kayaking, Ōkārito Lagoon and white heron nature reserve tours, Lake Mapourika kayaking tours.

Further reading: Aoraki/Mt Cook/Westland/Tai Poutini Parkmap; NZMS 260 series topographical map G35/H35; track brochures and route guides.

Special conditions: Ice collapse and rockfalls can occur any time at the terminal faces of the glaciers. Keep behind rope barriers and take note of park signs warning of changing conditions.

If crossing rivers on the beach, beware of quicksand and fast tidal flows.

Accommodation in the park's two townships is often full during the summer months, so it is advisable to make bookings well in advance.

Visitor centre: Westland/Tai Poutini National Park Visitor Centre in Franz Josef/Waiau village provides information on tracks and other activities within the park, an audiovisual and publication sales.

Westland/Tai Poutini National Park Visitor Centre
PO Box 14
Franz Josef/Waiau
Phone 0-3-752 0796
Email westlandnpvc@doc.govt.nz
Open daily 8.30 am to 6 pm (summer); 8.30 am to 1 pm and 12 pm to 4.45 pm (winter)

Mt Aspiring National Park

Location: south-western South Island

Features: mountains ▪ glaciers ▪ ice plateau ▪ vast river valleys ▪ beech forests ▪ subalpine meadows ▪ World Heritage Area

Activities: tramping ▪ short walks ▪ mountaineering ▪ ski-mountaineering ▪ jetboating ▪ scenic drives ▪ scenic flights ▪ hunting ▪ fishing

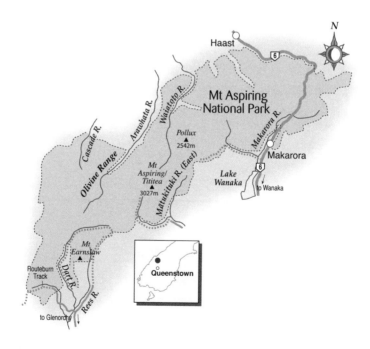

This park is one of the greatest areas of mountain wilderness in New Zealand. It is a major part of the 2,600,000 ha Te Wāhipounamu – South West New Zealand World Heritage Area.

The mountains, glaciers, snowfields, valleys and forests of the park straddle the Main Divide and sprawl across the southern end of the Southern Alps/Kā Tiritiri o te Moana. Dominating the landscape is Mt Aspiring/Tititea (3027 m), the highest and most glaciated mountain in New Zealand outside the Aoraki/Mt Cook region. Named Tititea ('glistening peak') by the Māori people, it soars skyward in a shape reminiscent of Switzerland's famous Matterhorn. It is undoubtedly one of New Zealand's classic summits.

Aside from many mountaineering challenges, the park has a plethora of valley tramping routes linked by mountain passes, including the Routeburn Track, a Great Walk that crosses into Fiordland. There are three major park entrance points: Glenorchy, Mātukituki Valley and Makarora, plus there is a massive area of untracked wilderness in the remote south-west of the park that requires days of foot travel to reach. In more accessible spots there are many short walks so that all visitors can explore the delightful landscape features around the fringes of the park. The Haast Highway is a stunning, scenic mountain drive.

About the park

Historically, the park region was devoid of human footprints but for those of Māori travellers, who visited seasonal hunting camps and crossed mountain passes to reach the West Coast pounamu (greenstone) fields. They were followed by European explorers, many making their way in the company of Māori guides.

Mt Aspiring/Tititea was first climbed in 1909, before mountaineers turned to other alpine peaks emanating from the Aspiring massif for new challenges. There is a huge choice of tramping routes: valley after valley of grassy river flats hemmed by mountains with beech forest covering their lower flanks, which lead to subalpine meadows, rocky cirques, waterfalls, glacial lakes and mountain passes.

In 1960 the completion of the highway over Haast Pass/Tioripatea opened up the park's northern splendour to visitors. Now tourists drive in coaches and campervans through this previously remote region of mountains, forests and deep river gorges where some 10,000 to 200,000 years ago, a massive glacier gouged its way across the rocky ridgeline to shape the ice-smoothed pass.

Ice and rock

Today the large Olivine Ice Plateau and the Volta and Bonar Glaciers dominate the park's high-altitude snowfields. However, these and a hundred other glaciers throughout the park are but tiny remnants of the massive ice sheets that once covered the region.

The imprint of ice is seen in landscapes throughout the park, from the glacier-honed summit of Mt Aspiring/Tititea, to the lakes, cirque basins, hanging valleys, moraines, U-shaped valleys and, to the east of the park, the deep troughs of Lakes Wakatipu and Wanaka.

The ice has carved its way predominantly through brittle schist rock made up of shining mica, quartz and feldspars. It is also easily eroded by wind and water, so the ice-sculptured landscapes are also characterised by huge scree slopes.

The Red Hills, in the south-western corner of the park, are a geological curiosity. These hills are made of ultramafic rocks, with high mineral contents of magnesium, iron and serpentine. The presence of similar Red Hills 500 km to the north, near Nelson, is a geological phenomenon attributed to the lateral displacement of the Alpine Fault. The striking Red Hills are notable for their barrenness: their oxide soils are too toxic for all but the hardiest plants.

The dramatic contrast between schist and ultramafic rock is clearly shown in the park at Simonin Pass, where the Livingston Fault draws a sharp line between red-coloured scree and schist slopes covered with silver beech forest.

Beeches, birds and above the bushline

Beech forests dominate the park; silver beech is most common in northern areas, while red beech is found to the south, particularly in the Routeburn and Dart valleys. The forests provide habitats for an impressive variety of native birds, including the South Island rifleman, brown creeper, South Island robin, kākā, yellow-crowned parakeet (kākāriki), wood pigeon, tui and a significant population of Haast tokoeka, a species of kiwi. The Mt Aspiring and Fiordland beech forests are the only places where endangered yellowheads survive in reasonable numbers, and research into predator control to sustain these populations is currently being undertaken in the red beech forests of the Dart Valley.

On the western side of the Main Divide, where the rainfall is nearly four times greater than the rain-shadowed eastern side, lowland silver beech forests are mixed with podocarps such as rimu, mataī, miro and kahikatea, and are filled with understorey shrubs, ferns and vines.

The park's subalpine 'gardens' rate among the country's most diverse. These communities flourish in the valley heads above the treeline, on rock outcrops, snow banks and in alpine bogs, while some hardy lichens survive even above the permanent snowline. The park contains tussocklands, shrublands and herbfields where the world's largest mountain buttercup, *Ranunculus lyallii*, *Celmisia* daisies and gentians are just some of the flowering delights.

These alpine regions are the domain of kea and tiny but resilient rock wrens, the only remaining species of the ancient New Zealand wren genus, which survive the harsh alpine winter by sheltering in rock crevices beneath the snow.

Since the park was established in 1964, it has nearly doubled in size. These significant additions have drawn more complete ecosystems under the umbrella of national park protection. More recently, topuni status has been established over areas especially significant to Ngāi Tahu people. This does not override park status, but ensures Ngāi Tahu values are recognised. In the park these include Pikirakatahi (Mt Earnslaw) and Te Koroka (Slip Stream).

What to do

Short walks

Thunder Creek Falls (Gates of Haast) 5 minutes return

Short but spectacular, this walk leads through mixed podocarp and beech forest to the thundering 28 m falls. It is located just downhill from the place the highway crosses the Haast River, near Haast Pass/Tioripatea. The sealed path is suitable for wheelchairs.

Blue Pool (near Makarora) 30 minutes return

Look for trout in this crystal-clear, aquamarine-coloured pool, encircled by a forested gorge at the mouth of the Blue River. The walk descends gently through beech forest and crosses the Makarora River by a long but sturdy swingbridge. Along the way listen for tūī, bellbirds and robins, and in late summer look for red-flowering mistletoe clinging to host trees. A tramping track leads a further 2 to 3 hours up the Blue Valley, to a small, open flat known as Camp Flat.

Bridle Track (Haast Pass/Tioripatea) 1.5 hours one way

Part of the original pack track over Haast Pass/Tioripatea, built around the 1870s and used by prospectors, surveyors and cattle drovers. The new Haast Highway makes a detour here, leaving this old, forest-lined trail for walkers to enjoy the mountain landscapes and marvel at the navigational and construction feats of those earlier travellers. Start at the western end, closer to the pass, to enjoy a downhill wander (you'll need to organise a vehicle pick-up or walk both ways). Note the contrasting colours of the blue-green Fish River, just before it joins the milky, glacier-fed Makarora River.

Lake Sylvan (near Glenorchy) 45 minutes one way

An easy, mainly level walking track through red beech forest to this glacier-formed lake. Forest and wetland birds are usually abundant.

An old tramline is a legacy of short-lived efforts to mill the native beech trees during the 1920s and 1930s.

Longer walks

Rob Roy Valley (Mātukituki Valley) 4 to 5 hours return

A delightful mountain walk, taking in river flats, beech forest, subalpine herbfields and flowers, waterfalls, and a glacier and snowfields. The track starts on open flats, crosses the West Mātukituki River by swingbridge, leads through beech forest in the lower Rob Roy Valley, then climbs briefly to open subalpine herbfields. Here the views are impressive: waterfalls plunging over cliffs topped with broken blue ice. Glaciers, snowfield and the 2606 m Rob Roy Peak tower above.

Aspiring Hut (Mātukituki Valley) 2.5 hours one way

Follows the open valley floor of the West Mātukituki River, which is lined by snow-capped mountains, to a historic and rather grand stone hut. The West Mātukituki has long been an access route for climbing Mt Aspiring/Tititea and other nearby mountains, and this hut was built by the New Zealand Alpine Club in 1949. It is now available for public use. The peak of Mt Aspiring/Tititea can just be seen from the hut, above and beyond mountains at the head of the valley. The lower West Mātukituki is pastoral farmland, outside the park boundary.

Routeburn Flats (near Glenorchy) 2 hours one way

The first part of the Routeburn Track Great Walk climbs gently through beech forest and beside the lower Routeburn River to some fine mountain scenery. The track passes several side streams that can run fast and deep in heavy rain, climbs beside the rocky canyons of the Routeburn Gorge, then emerges onto the open, grassy Routeburn Flats. Here is mountain scenery at its best. The flats are surrounded by mountain faces and, looking to the head of the valley, Routeburn Falls plunge steeply from the U-shaped upper Routeburn Valley. Routeburn Flats Hut is 10 minutes' walk across the flats, and if the weather is clear Routeburn Falls Hut can be seen high on a mountain ledge beside the Routeburn Falls.

Mt Brewster Hut (Haast Highway) 3 to 4 hours one way
A steep but rewarding climb first through beech forest, then up a snow-tussock face to a rocky ridgeline that leads to little Mt Brewster Hut (4 bunks), nestled beside a mountain tarn 45 minutes from the bushline. There are views of the highest mountains in the park, including Mt Aspiring/Tititea. If staying overnight, it is a superb setting in which to watch the sunset.

Multi-day tramping trips
The park is blessed with natural valley routes. Most of these routes are seasonal: in winter many passes become impassable except by trampers with specialist expertise and equipment. Following is a selection of the most popular tramping trips in the park. Except for the Routeburn Track, these trips require a reasonable ability to navigate in the back country. Most range from tramping tracks to routes marked by occasional signs or poles.

Routeburn Track 2 to 3 days
Passes from Mt Aspiring National Park to Fiordland National Park through a stunning array of alpine landscapes: mountains, tussock-lands, alpine herbfields, streams, tarns, lakes and waterfalls, glacial valleys and rainforest. There are four huts and camping is permitted only at the two campsites. There is also a guided walk option that uses two private lodges. Transport will need to be arranged – though the track is only 33 km long, the two ends are 350 km apart by road.

Much of the track is above the bushline and exposed to changeable weather. In winter there is extreme avalanche danger and much of the track is likely to be covered by heavy snow. The track can be walked in combination with the adjoining Caples and Greenstone Tracks, which explore two valleys next to Fiordland National Park.

A day in the life of a hut warden

Te Ānau resident Pat Craw has been working as a hut warden on national park tracks for the past 13 years, specifically on the Routeburn, Milford, Hollyford and Kepler Tracks.

The best part of the job, she says, is meeting so many interesting people from all over the world. 'I find I can learn so much. I usually have an atlas with me in the hut so I can look up where people are from. The only sad thing is I wish I could get to know them better. After a night they move on and the next lot comes along.'

The other wonderful thing for Pat is the plant life. 'I know where all the alpine flowers are and I get to see them flowering in sequence throughout the summer. Every time I come back after a few days off there will be some new plants flowering.'

Nevertheless, life as a hut warden is not all about chatting with people and watching the flowers grow. Pat's day starts around 7 am with a radio schedule, checking details like the weather forecast. Then she 'sorts out the people', advising them about the track ahead and the weather, sometimes suggesting they wait an hour or so for the weather to clear. When they have all left she cleans the hut, the benches, cooking units, heating units, bunkrooms, floors, veranda and surrounds, by which time it's usually lunchtime.

The afternoons are spent in various ways, carrying out hut and track maintenance or perhaps finding time for a walk to enjoy those alpine flowers. By mid afternoon the new lot of walkers will start to arrive, along with their multitude of questions. Pat says she never tires of answering the same questions over and over again, because the people are all so different.

In the evening she'll give a hut talk about what to expect the following day: weather, track conditions, special features to look out for, bird life – and of course the flowers. Her last job is turning out the lights at around 10 pm, leaving not a lot of time before she starts yet another day.

Rees/Dart Track 4 to 5 days

Two park valleys linked by an alpine pass (Rees Saddle). Features are open valleys, great mountain and glacier scenery, alpine vegetation and the presence of less common bird species, including the endangered yellowhead. The lower valleys pass through Crown lease grazing runs.

This 77 km track is longer, steeper and more challenging than the Routeburn Track and requires a high standard of fitness. Most days average 6 to 8 hours' tramping. The alpine section, around Rees Saddle, is subject to avalanches in late winter and spring.

There are three park huts and hut wardens are present from November to April. Trampers should carry cooking stoves. Camping is permitted, except in the fragile alpine and subalpine areas of Rees Saddle between Shelter Rock Hut and Dart Hut. In winter the upper valleys will be covered by snow and the round trip is feasible only by suitably experienced and equipped climbers.

The trip starts near Glenorchy (1 hour's drive from Queenstown). Tramper shuttle transport to each valley is available, and it is possible to organise jetboat transport to the lower Dart Valley.

Gillespie Pass 3 to 4 days

This 58 km tramp begins at Makarora and takes in three valleys (the Wilkin, Siberia and Young) and an alpine pass. It features a delightful mix of wide grassy flats, subalpine herbfields and snow-tussock basins, mountain faces that stream with waterfalls after heavy rain, beech forests and clear mountain rivers.

There are two huts (Young and Siberia) and a campsite in the lower Young Valley with open shelter, toilets and fireplace. This is not a winter trip and should be undertaken by relatively experienced tramping parties. Tracks vary from marked walking tracks to poled routes. Even in summer the alpine section over Gillespie Pass is subject to poor visibility, heavy rain, wind and snow.

River crossings are required to start each end of this round trip, though jetboat access can be arranged from Makarora to Kerin Forks, in the Wilkin River, reducing the walking by 6 to 7 hours. Jetboat transport is also available across the Makarora River to the Young Valley if the river is too high to ford. From November to April a radio is installed at the Young River mouth that links with the Makarora Visitor Centre so trampers can order a boat if the river is too high to cross. It is also possible to fly by small fixed-wing plane from Makarora to a grass airstrip in Siberia Valley.

Wilkin Valley 2 to 3 days

A classic tramping valley, with easy walking along wide river flats and stunning mountain scenery all around. There are delightful side trips possible into several tributary valleys. At the head of the valley's north branch there are three glacier-formed lakes, nestled amidst high alpine basins and glacial moraines covered with alpine herbfields. From Makarora to the valley head is a total of about 12 to 14 hours' walking. Access involves crossing the Makarora River, which is feasible at low river flows – seek advice about fording channels from Makarora park staff. Travel up the valley also involves some crossings of the Wilkin River, which might be impossible depending on river levels. There are two huts (Kerin Forks and Top Forks) in the valley.

It is possible to travel up the valley by jetboat to Kerin Forks (saving 6 to 7 hours' walking), or fly by small plane to an airstrip at Jumboland (1 hour's walk from Top Forks Hut at the head of the valley).

West Mātukituki Valley 2 to 3 days

One of the park's most popular tramping valleys, the West Mātukituki is also a major approach route for climbers heading for Mt Aspiring/ Tititea and other mountaineering challenges. The lower valley track traverses open pastoral farmland and some beech forest alongside the Mātukituki River, and is lined on both sides by some of the park's highest mountains. Close to the park boundary the historic Aspiring Hut (2 to 3 hours) is a good base for further explorations. The time spent in the valley is dependent on how many side trips people choose to take, though many of these climb steep, slippery routes that even in summer are suitable only for experienced trampers.

From Mt Aspiring Hut it is a further 1.5 hours to Pearl Flat, then a

Top tips

- The best time for tramping in the park is late summer (March/ April). There is generally more stable weather, fewer people around and no snow melt so the rivers are lower, making tramping access easier.
- If travelling on the Haast Highway, take time for the short walks to Thunder Falls (sealed and suitable for wheelchairs) and Blue Pool.
- If time or fitness prevents a longer trip, walk to the Routeburn Flats, the first 2 hours of the Routeburn Track, for a grand, 'surrounded by mountains' experience.
- The walk to Rob Roy Valley, in the West Mātukituki, leads to superb mountain environment, an alpine basin that's surrounded by bluffs, snowfields and glaciers.
- A recommended summer tramping trip for those reasonably fit and experienced is Gillespie Pass. Three valleys, one alpine pass, a classic trip.

very steep 2 to 3 hour climb to French Ridge (formerly Lucas Trotter) Hut, which sits above the bushline but below the normal summertime snowline. In summer this is a tramping route, though the upper section is particularly exposed in bad weather. From Pearl Flat a further 2 hours' walking leads to the head of the valley, though avalanche danger exists here from around June to November.

Cascade Saddle 4 to 5 days

An often used but potentially treacherous summer alpine route, from the park's West Mātukituki Valley to the upper Dart Valley. Very steep snow-tussock slopes around bluffs on Cascade Saddle become deceptively slippery when wet or covered with snow; this can happen even in summer. The climb to the bushline is straightforward, but the actual crossing of the saddle is regarded as one of the more difficult routes in the area. The track climbs from Mt Aspiring Hut, in the West Mātukituki Valley, up and around steep bluffs and snow tussock to Cascade Saddle. (Those heading in the opposite direction must find the pylon that marks the descent through the bluffs. It is much harder to go down this route than up.) The route from Mt Aspiring Hut, which passes to the south of the saddle, follows orange standards and then rock cairns as it descends, once again on steep and slippery slopes, to the Dart Valley floor. From here there is a choice of walking down the Dart Valley, or climbing Rees Saddle and walking the Rees Valley.

Olivine Wilderness Area

Over 80,000 ha, a quarter of the park, is designated as the Olivine Wilderness Area. In the remote south-west of the park, it straddles 60 km of the Main Divide and protects glaciers, mountains, remote valleys, unruly rivers and diverse wildlife habitats. No huts, tracks or aircraft landings are permitted – the area can be visited only on nature's terms.

Mountaineering

While the classic Mt Aspiring/Tititea is the drawcard for many climbers, there are many other peaks and mountain ranges throughout the park that provide challenging and rewarding climbs in remote wilderness country. In fact, the park straddles the Main Divide and has more than a hundred peaks over 2000 m. Evocative names bestowed on them by early explorers, such as Stargazer, Moonraker, Cloudmaker, Castor, Pollux and Apollo, convey the esteem commanded by these lofty peaks. The Māori name Tititea, 'glistening peak', is equally telling.

Mt Aspiring/Tititea was first climbed in 1909 via the south-west face. The first north-west ridge ascent was made in 1913. Many of today's climbers base themselves at Colin Todd Hut, below the north-west ridge. Climbers should note that even the approach routes to the hut, climbing out of the head of the West Mātukituki Valley, are challenging and require mountaineering expertise and equipment. Helicopter access is available, but to keep intrusive noise away landings are restricted to Bevan Col. Depending on snow conditions on the Bonar Glacier, the col is 30 minutes' to 2 hours' walk from Colin Todd Hut.

The availability of any helicopter access at all is the subject of debate among climbers, many of whom advocate the purist tradition of approaching mountain climbs by multi-day tramps up access valleys.

Mt Earnslaw (2819 m), the second-highest mountain in the park, stands between the popular tramping valleys of the Rees and the Dart; it was first climbed in 1890. Other mountains extend from the Forbes and Barrier Ranges in the south to Mt Brewster near Haast Pass/Tiori-patea. In the remote western regions lie the Haast Range and the vast, glacial wilderness region of the Olivine Range and ice plateau.

Professional climbing guides lead guided ascents and beginner and advanced climbing courses in the park. The New Zealand Alpine Club provides a guide to climbing routes.

Ski-mountaineering

There are very few ski-mountaineering opportunities in the park during winter. They occur mainly on the Bonar Glacier, where helicopter access is possible to Bevan Col, and to a lesser extent on the more remote Brewster Glacier.

Fishing

Introduced brown and rainbow trout are present in park rivers. Fishing licences are available from local sports shops and online at www.fishandgame.org.nz. Guided fishing trips are also available in the park. Some guides are licensed to take fishing parties into designated remote areas by helicopter.

Hunting

Recreational hunting for introduced red deer, whitetail deer and chamois is encouraged in the park. Hunting permits are available from park visitor centres. Hunting is not permitted in the Routeburn Valley, or in the Dart Valley south of Chinamans Bluff.

Scenic flights

For the less able or adventurous, exploration of the park's mountains, valleys and glaciers by scenic flight reveals the extent of glaciation and permanent snowfields and is a memorable experience. Flights are available from Makarora, Wanaka and Queenstown.

Haast Highway

One of New Zealand's premier mountain drives traverses the north of the park as it crosses the Main Divide at Haast Pass/Tioripatea. This is the lowest of the three road passes linking the west and east coasts, and it travels through contrasting landscapes. As it passes from west to east vegetation changes notably, from luxuriant rainforests featuring tall rimu and kahikatea in the west, to drier beech forests in the east, mixed with open, grassy river flats. There are occasional tantalising glimpses into park valleys, and an ever-present mountain backdrop. To the east of the park boundary the highway continues along the shores of the neighbouring lakes of Wanaka and Hāwea, with the park's mountains remaining an impressive background.

The 140 km road is sealed and remains open throughout the year, except for during occasional heavy snowfalls in winter. Several short walks and information panels provide an insight to scenic and historic features along the highway. There are picnic areas and four self-registration park campsites. Visitor centres at Wanaka, Makarora and Haast offer up-to-date information on road conditions and features.

Information

Getting there: From the West Coast the Haast Highway (SH6) traverses the northern fringes of the park. Glenorchy, entrance to the southern end, is 48 km from Queenstown. The Mātukituki Valley entrance is 54 km from Wanaka. There are daily bus services to Wanaka, Queenstown and the West Coast, and daily flights to Queenstown and Wanaka. Shuttle services are available for trampers and mountaineers to the park's main access points. Jetboat access can be arranged to the Dart and Wilkin Valleys and across the Makarora River, and small-plane and helicopter access is available to some areas of the park.

When to go: Any time for short walks and scenic flights. Summer/autumn for tramping and climbing, winter for ski-mountaineering.

Climate: Changeable. Usually settled in late summer. Stormy weather likely in spring and autumn. High rainfall, particularly on the western side. Summers mild, winters cold and frosty, with snow to low levels. Permanent snow above 2000 m.

Accommodation and facilities: There is a range of backpacker, motel, camping, homestay and luxury lodge accommodation in or near the townships of Glenorchy, Makarora and Haast, plus cafés, a few shops and fuel. A full range of accommodation, restaurants, shops and services is offered in the busy, international tourist towns of Queenstown and Wanaka. There are four self-registration park campsites along the Haast Highway.

Commercial ventures: Guided climbing, walking, fishing and hunting are available, along with scenic flights and heli-hikes. Scenic jetboat tours are available in the Dart and Wilkin Rivers. Tramper transport can be arranged by bus, jetboat, small plane and helicopter.

Further reading: Mt Aspiring Parkmap; NZMS 260 series topographical maps D39, D40, E38, E39, E40, F37, F38, F39, G37, G38; park brochures and fact sheets; The *Mt Aspiring Region: A Guide for Mountaineers*, Allan Uren and Mark Watson (New Zealand Alpine Club); *Moir's Guide North*, Geoff Spearpoint (New Zealand Alpine Club); *Land Aspiring: The Story of Mount Aspiring National Park*, Neville Peat.

Special conditions: Many valley routes that involve alpine passes are summer trips only. Snow and avalanche risk make the routes extremely dangerous. Year-round, any route above the bushline can be subject to adverse weather: heavy rain, poor visibility, high winds and snow.

Many valley routes involve unbridged river crossings. Never attempt to cross a river in flood. Be prepared to wait for as long as it takes for the river to drop.

Sandflies are abundant!

Visitor centres: Park visitor centres at Wanaka, Makarora and Glenorchy offer information, weather updates, brochures, maps, hut tickets and hunting permits. There are also displays about natural and historic features of the park. There are i-SITE visitor centres in Wanaka and Queenstown, where information and bookings for commercial ventures in the park are available.

Wanaka Visitor Centre
Ardmore Street
PO Box 93
Wanaka
Phone 0-3-443 7660
Email wanakavc@doc.govt.nz
Open daily 8 am to 5 pm
(summer); shorter hours
during winter

Makarora Visitor Centre
Haast Highway 6
Makarora
Private Bag
Via Wanaka
Phone 0-3-443 8365
Email makaroravc@doc.govt.nz
Open daily 8 am to 5 pm
(summer); shorter hours
during winter

Glenorchy Visitor Centre
Cnr Mull and Oban Streets
PO Box 2
Glenorchy
Phone 0-3-442 9937
Email glenorchyvc@doc.govt.nz
Open daily 8.30 am to 4.30 pm
(summer); closed during winter

Fiordland National Park

Location: south-west corner of the South Island

Features: World Heritage Area ∎ fiords ∎ mountains ∎ lakes and rivers ∎ vast forests ∎ New Zealand's largest wilderness

Activities: short walks ∎ tramping ∎ climbing ∎ diving ∎ sea and lake kayaking ∎ scenic cruises and flights ∎ birdwatching ∎ natural heritage tours ∎ hunting ∎ fishing ∎ mountain biking

Fiordland is one of the great natural areas of the world. Its 1,200,000 ha include a fiord-indented coastline, glaciated mountains, lakes, rivers and the largest continuous tract of native forest in the country.

The park covers the south-western corner of the South Island. It is New Zealand's largest and the world's fifth-largest national park, and is a major part of Te Wāhipounamu – South West New Zealand World Heritage Area. Within Fiordland are the world-renowned tourist destinations of Milford Sound/Piopiotahi and Doubtful Sound/Patea, plus the Milford, Routeburn and Kepler Great Walks.

Although much of the park is wilderness, tourism services enable people of all fitness levels to experience its natural splendour. Each year thousands of visitors enjoy cruises on the lakes and fiords, coach tours along the Milford Road, scenic flights, nature tours, short walks and guided walks. For the more adventurous, the park presents a challenging menu of tramping, mountaineering, hunting, kayaking and diving. Te Ānau township is the main entrance point to the park.

About the park

Three key factors have shaped Fiordland: tectonic uplift, glaciation and the ancient, hard rock of its mountains. Unlike in other, erosion-prone South Island mountains, the hard crystalline and metamorphic rocks of Fiordland have resisted erosion and the landscape is little changed since great glaciers shaped the fiords, lakes and U-shaped valleys so characteristic of the park.

Fiords (erroneously called sounds) are found in only a few places around the world. In Fiordland, glaciers flowing west from the mountains gouged deep trenches that have since been flooded by the sea and formed the fiords that give the park its name. Fourteen fiords indent over 1000 km of remote coastline. They penetrate deep into the mountains, 30 to 40 km in length, up to 500 m deep and bounded by sheer walls that reach a staggering 1.5 km in height. Reportedly the world's highest sea cliff is Mitre Peak, which rises 1700 m sheer from the water of Milford Sound/Piopiotahi.

These fiords support a unique marine environment, including the world's biggest and shallowest population of black coral. Two marine reserves protect small portions of this environment. More special inhabitants live above the surface, such as one of the world's rarest penguins, the endemic Fiordland crested penguin. However, this timid penguin is rarely seen; visitors cruising the fiords are more likely to encounter dolphins, such as the pod of bottle-nosed dolphins that live in Doubtful Sound/Patea, fur seals or some of the myriad sea birds that thrive in this remote coastal environment.

East-flowing glaciers gouged the basins filled now by lakes. Of these Te Ānau is the biggest, Manapōuri arguably the most beautiful, Hauroko the deepest and Pōteriteri the most remote. These magnificent lakes form the eastern boundary of the park and are the major access points.

Lake Manapōuri has a special place in the history of conservation in New Zealand. In the 1970s a plan to raise the lake's level for hydro-electricity generation was thwarted by a concerted conservation campaign, the first of its kind in this country.

Water

Water dominates Fiordland. The lakes, fiords, rivers and waterfalls of the park are constantly replenished by one of the wettest climates found anywhere in the world. This is not necessarily a deterrent to park visitors, though floods, avalanches and snowfalls can at times interrupt travel in the park. From a safe distance, the sight of massive volumes of water cascading down mountain walls is a true Fiordland experience, not to be missed.

Fiordland's rainforests thrive in such a climate. Most dominant is beech, the dark tree-trunks often wreathed with lichens, mosses and filmy ferns. But the great podocarps are also present and there is an enormous range of vegetation types, including wetlands, estuaries,

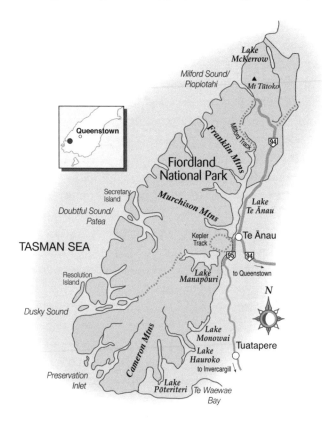

dunes, subalpine shrublands, tussockfields and alpine herbfields. There are few places in the temperate world where glaciers and alpine herbfields are found just 5 km away from densely forested coastlines, as is the case in the mountains near the mouth of Milford Sound/ Piopiotahi.

Plants and animals

Fiordland is home to large numbers of endemic and threatened plants and animals. Some 30 plant species are found only in Fiordland, 300 of the total 3000 insect species in the park are also endemic and there are significant populations of endemic snails, lizards and skinks. All Fiordland visitors are bound to come across namu, the pesky sandfly!

One of the most special of all the native species remaining in Fiordland is the endangered takahē, the large, flightless rail thought to be extinct until it was rediscovered in a remote tussock valley in 1948. About 150 takahē now live here, while others have been relocated to island sanctuaries to improve the bird's chances of survival.

Several bird species now rarely seen in other parts of New Zealand have survived in bigger populations in the great Fiordland wilderness. Observant park visitors may chance sightings of yellowheads, kākāriki, New Zealand falcons and South Island robins. Brown teal and blue ducks live in the park's rivers and streams; southern tokoeka, the kiwi species that inhabits Rakiura, are reasonably common; and the kea is likely to make its presence known.

People in the park

The very physical nature of rugged, remote Fiordland has thwarted large-scale human settlement. Nevertheless, Māori stories and place names for features throughout the park (though not all acknowledged on present-day maps) tell of these people's strong association with the region. Archaeological evidence points to pre-1800 Māori dwellings in southern coastline areas. Further north, the Milford Track was once a route commonly used by Māori to reach the valuable pounamu (greenstone) of Milford Sound/Piopiotahi.

According to Māori, the great fiords were created by legendary ancestor Tū Te Rakiwhānoa, who carved them from the hard mountain rock with his bare hands. He started in the south, leaving ragged coastlines and many islands. As he moved north his technique improved, so by the time he reached Piopiotahi he carved the perfect, steep-sided fiord that attracts the tourists today. But a second legendary figure, Hine nui te po, decided Tū Te Rakiwhānoa had become too vain about his work, so to teach him a lesson introduced namu, the sandfly. Park visitors today should be warned. Namu has millions of descendants!

The first European arrivals included British explorer James Cook, then sealers, whalers, surveyors and prospectors brought a flurry of activity around the Fiordland coast.

Tourism

The grandeur of Fiordland has long been a drawcard for international tourists. Work began on developing the now famous Milford Track as long ago as 1888. The Milford, Routeburn, Kepler and Hollyford Tracks are extremely popular and attract tens of thousands of walkers each year. Most have a booking system during summer months. There is also a host of other impressive tramping options (a network encompassing 500 km of track and some 60 huts), plus many shorter walks that explore the forests, glacial lakes, waterfalls and alpine tarns.

In the north of the park, the Darran Mountains are known for rock-climbing routes, and Fiordland's highest mountain, Tūtoko (2746 m), is one of several snow-climbing challenges in the region.

Many of the park's visitors experience the might of Fiordland without stepping onto a forest track. The Milford Road, which carves through some of the park's highest mountains via the Homer Tunnel, is acknowledged as one of the most stunning scenic drives in the world. A frenetic scenic flight schedule makes little Milford airstrip the busiest airfield in the country, while thousands more tourists opt for launch cruises on mountain-flanked lakes and fiords.

Conservation and tourism have happily coexisted since Fiordland National Park was established in 1952. Half a million people now visit the park each year, yet there are still some remote parts of this vast wilderness where no human foot has ever stepped.

What to do

Short walks

Following is a selection of the many short walks that explore a range of landscapes and are suitable for a variety of ages and fitness levels. Park brochures contain a full list.

Ivon Wilson Park and Te Ānau Wildlife Centre (Te Ānau)
40 minutes loop

A pleasant interlude on Fiordland's fringes, beside Lake Te Ānau. In Ivon Wilson Park walkers can enjoy 35 ha of native and exotic plantings, great Fiordland views, plus a picturesque lake stocked with trout as a child's fishery (licences available at the visitor centre). The wildlife centre is home to many native birds including tūī, kākāriki, kākā, kea and one of New Zealand's most endangered species, takahē.

Rainbow Reach to Shallow Bay (Te Ānau) 3 hours return
An easy section of the Kepler Track, through beech forest to Lake Manapōuri, with a great view of the mountain-framed lake. Park huts Moturau and Shallow Bay offer shelter and toilets on the lake edge.

Mirror Lakes (Milford Road) 5 minutes return
Beautiful reflective views of the Earl Mountains. Wetland plants and birds are abundant. The path is suitable for wheelchairs.

Lake Gunn Nature Walk (Milford Road) 45 minutes loop

A gentle meander through red-beech forest, taking in lakeside beaches. Look for forest birds, including the endangered whitehead. The path is suitable for wheelchairs.

The Chasm (Milford Road) 20 minutes return

Dramatic views of sculptured rock canyons and waterfalls in the Cleddau River, near Milford Sound/Piopiotahi.

Milford Sound Foreshore Walk: Te Paepae Tirohanga o Piopiotahi (Milford Sound/Piopiotahi) 20 minutes return

A walk away from the Sound's tourism development that has some of the most spectacular views at Milford. Information panels explain the special fiord environment and invite walkers to explore the foreshore habitat. The path is suitable for wheelchairs.

Longer walks

Key Summit (Milford Road) 3 hours return

A steady though well-graded climb to outstanding outlooks of the Humboldt and Darran mountains (Fiordland's highest) and the glacier-gouged Hollyford Valley. The walk follows the Fiordland end of the Routeburn Track for an hour, then branches and climbs for 20 minutes to Key Summit, a delightful boardwalked area of tarns and bogs where there is a self-guided alpine nature walk. Shelter and toilets are at Howden Hut, 20 minutes further along the Routeburn Track from the Key Summit turn-off.

Gertrude Saddle (Milford Road) 4 to 5 hours return

A steady climb over open, subalpine and rocky terrain to a mountain saddle, with a stunning view into Milford Sound/Piopiotahi. The route is marked by poles, exposed to the elements and suitable for people with appropriate experience and equipment.

Lake Marian (Hollyford Valley) 3 hours return

Signposted at a car park about 1 km down the Hollyford Road, the track meanders for 20 minutes through silver-beech forest to a series of waterfalls, then climbs steeply to the bushline and a view of Lake Marian. Nestled in a hanging valley, the lake is framed by and reflects the sheer granite walls of the Darran Mountains.

Circle Track (Manapōuri) 3 hours loop

This route is moderately steep, with boat transport required to cross the Waiau River (a dinghy can be hired from Manapōuri store). The track climbs through beech forest to excellent lookouts of Hope Arm, the Garnock Burn, Lake Manapōuri and surrounding mountains.

Multi-day tramping trips

Park publications provide comprehensive track descriptions and details on booking systems, transport and special conditions for the most popular of these tracks. During the Great Walks season (late October to late April) hut bookings are essential for the Milford, Routeburn and Kepler Tracks and huts are supplied with wardens, gas cooking and lighting and radio contact with Department of Conservation staff. Bookings can be made from July.

Milford Track 4 days

Often referred to as the finest walk in the world, this famous track traverses two glacial valleys and crosses an alpine pass, linking the northern arm of Lake Te Ānau with Milford Sound/Piopiotahi. Summer-flowering alpine plants, waterfalls, the companionship of kea and bush birds complement the grandeur of the mountains.

During the Great Walks season all travel starts from the Lake Te Ānau end. Numbers are limited and walkers are advised to book well in advance. No camping is permitted. There is also a guided walk option using private lodges. Outside of the Great Walks season the 53.5 km track is extremely avalanche prone and ice and snow are likely to make travel on Mackinnon Pass hazardous. Throughout the year, the weather can be extremely changeable. Heavy rain is a regular occurrence. Access to the track involves boat transport across Lake Te Ānau and across Milford Sound/Piopiotahi.

Routeburn Track 2 to 3 days

The Routeburn Track passes through Fiordland and Aspiring National Parks. Details of this Great Walk can be found on page 168.

Kepler Track 3 to 4 days

Easily accessible from Te Ānau township, the 60 km Kepler Track climbs from the shore of Lake Te Ānau to the open, subalpine terrain of Mt Luxmore, crosses a spectacular but exposed alpine ridge then descends the Iris Burn Valley into beech forest and to the shores of Lake Manapōuri. It features stunning outlooks of central Fiordland's mountains and lakes. There are three huts and camping is permitted only at the two designated campsites. The alpine ridge section, between Luxmore and Iris Burn huts, can be extremely difficult in bad weather, with high winds, driving rain and sleet likely. During winter the track is likely to be impassable as a through route because of snow. There is also high avalanche risk. Walking in and out of the lower sections is a safer and pleasant option.

Hollyford Track 4 days

Follows the Hollyford Valley through beech and coastal rainforest and around Lake McKerrow to the coast at isolated Martins Bay. Although framed by Fiordland's highest mountains, this is a low-altitude track that can be walked in any season. At any time of the year, however, heavy rain can cause flooding and tree falls. Air access can be arranged to or from Martins Bay and, during summer, jetboat transport across Lake McKerrow can be prearranged (reducing the walking time by up to a day). On the 56 km track there are six park huts, which operate on a first-come, first-served basis. During summer it would pay to carry a tent. Camping is permitted. There is also a guided option, using private lodges.

Manapōuri Tracks

A small network of low-level tracks in beech forest around the south-east corner of Lake Manapōuri. They feature charming outlooks of the Fiordland mountains across what is regarded as one the most beautiful lakes in New Zealand. There are two huts and camping is permitted. Boat transport across the Waiau River at Manapōuri can be arranged in the township.

Dusky Track 8 to 10 days

An 84 km exploration of remote southern Fiordland, traversing three major river valleys, crossing two mountain ranges, and linking Lake Manapōuri and Lake Hauroko, with a possible 2 day detour to Dusky Sound. The track can flood after heavy rain, and trampers can expect to encounter tree falls, deep mud and river crossings. There are 21 three-wire bridges. An exposed, alpine section between the Seaforth Valley and Lake Hauroko is likely to be impassable in winter and spring. Trampers must be experienced and equipped for the conditions and should sign a park intentions form. Carrying a mountain radio or personal locater beacon is recommended. Access is via Lake Manapōuri (daily boat service) or Lake Hauroko (scheduled boat service) or by chartered floatplane from Lake Hauroko or Dusky Sound to Te Ānau. There are eight park huts and camping is permitted. A shorter option is tramping one way from Lake Manapōuri (West Arm) to Supper Cove (Dusky Sound), incorporating boat and floatplane transport.

Hump Ridge Track 3 days

A 53 km circuit track taking in sandstone tors, coastal marine terraces, subalpine tarns and herbfields, plus two historic railway viaducts, all at the very southern tip of Fiordland. Unlike other tracks in New Zealand's national parks, Hump Ridge was developed in 2001 as a community venture in association with the Department of Conservation. Guided or independent walking is available, transport to and from Tuatapere township is provided, as are two huts with hot showers. Added options are ensuite accommodation and helicopter pack transport. Bookings are essential at www.humpridgetrack.co.nz.

Working together for conservation

Two special native species, bottle-nosed dolphins and blue ducks, are getting special treatment in Fiordland thanks to joint efforts by local tourism companies and conservation staff.

Dolphins first. Tour operators, conservation staff and local Māori people have banded together to ensure the long-term well-being of bottle-nosed dolphins in Doubtful Sound/Patea and Milford Sound/Piopiotahi. A liaison group has been established to undertake research and education and to develop a code of practice to help guide marine-mammal watching in Fiordland. The aim is to safeguard the dolphins and ensure the magic of an encounter with them can be experienced by generations to come.

The Department of Conservation administers regulations to manage and monitor the fast-growing whale- and dolphin-watching industry in New Zealand. It has been conducting major research assessing the impact of tourist vessels on the behaviour of marine mammals and the Fiordland dolphin research is an important component of this.

And then to the endangered blue duck. Populations are getting a boost from a Department of Conservation stoat-trapping programme being carried out by Milford Sound/Piopiotahi tour operators. Research shows that stoats, which eat eggs and chicks, are the biggest threat to the blue duck, a unique species of waterfowl that has no close relative anywhere in the world.

Blue ducks inhabit fast-moving mountain rivers and their numbers are in serious decline. However, several years of stoat trapping along the Milford Track and in the neighbouring Cleddau Valley, together with the captive rearing of eggs produced in the wild, has resulted in increased numbers of young blue ducks.

Particularly satisfying was the release in 2004 of three captive-reared ducklings into the headwaters of the Clinton River, on the Milford Track. The ducklings had been hatched from eggs that were rescued, along with their mother, from a nest in the path of an avalanche the previous year.

Trampers in the park can help. Knowing where the blue ducks are and that they are safe is an essential part of the recovery programme. Track walkers, or any visitors to any national park in fact, are asked to report sightings to conservation staff. Details including location and numbers, and the colours of any leg bands they might be wearing, are particularly useful.

Climbing

The steep, hard granite of the Darran Mountains offers some of New Zealand's finest rock climbing. Mt Tūtoko (2756 m) is the park's highest point and only major snow and ice climb. The Darrans can be approached via Gertrude Saddle (near Homer Tunnel), Tūtoko Valley and the lower Hollyford Valley. The climbing here is regarded as challenging, suitable only for experienced and competent climbers. March is the best time for climbing in the Darrans. No professional climbing guides are available in Fiordland.

Kayaking

Fiordland's glacial lakes and fiords, bounded by sheer mountains walls with waterfalls cascading, or by verdant beech or coastal rainforests, set the scene for some remote and stunning kayaking trips. In the fiords fur seals, penguins and dolphins will likely be your companions. The park's most popular kayaking destinations are Milford Sound/Piopiotahi, Lake Manapōuri and Doubtful Sound/Patea.

Several operators run guided trips, providing all equipment and offering day or multi-day trips. Kayaks can also be hired in Manapōuri and Te Ānau.

Diving

Fiordland is one of the few places in the world where centuries-old black corals and vivid red hydrocorals live in shallow water. A freshwater layer, pouring in from Fiordland's massive annual rainfall, overlies the seawater and filters out light, allowing deepwater species to live close to the surface. This phenomenon is known as deepwater emergence. It means the corals, along with a multitude of other marine animals, live at depths of less than 20 m on or beside the mountain walls that plunge beneath the surface directly to the floor of the fiords. Diving tours, with PADI-qualified operators, are available in Milford Sound/Piopiotahi. Visibility in the clear, relatively warm fiords is often up to 10 m. Also in Milford Sound/Piopiotahi, a deepwater observatory allows non-divers a glimpse of underwater life in Piopiotahi Marine Reserve.

Cruising

In Fiordland boats are the best way to get around. Boat travel on the lakes and fiords is also wonderfully scenic, so it follows that there is a plethora of cruising choices in the park. These range from short scenic trips that leave from popular road-ends, to multi-day wilderness cruises that explore Fiordland's remote fiords and coastline.

Of the shorter options, most popular are cruises in Milford Sound/Piopiotahi, across Lake Te Ānau to visit the Te Ānau Caves or exploring the lake by ketch, and an excellent, day-long boat/bus combination that takes you to both Lake Manapōuri and Doubtful Sound/Patea.

Longer cruises are offered in a variety of motor and sailing vessels, some more salubrious than others and many built especially for Fiordland conditions. Most feature expansive viewing decks, private or shared cabins, on-board nature guides, and tender craft and kayaks for shore explorations.

Jetboats and other boats are available for tours and water taxi transport on Lake Hauroko, Wairaurāhiri River, Lake Te Ānau, Lake Manapōuri and Lake McKerrow in the Hollyford Valley.

By air

Whether it's a scenic flight or being transported to or from a tramping, hunting, fishing or photography expedition, flying above the mountains, lakes and fiords of Fiordland can be a majestic experience. Small fixed-wing planes, floatplanes and helicopters offer scenic flights over most areas of Fiordland and other adjacent national parks. Most flight companies are Te Ānau based or fly from Queenstown. Milford Sound/Piopiotahi is a notable drawcard – in summer in particular

---

Top tips

- Key Summit is one of the best short walks in the country. Beech forest, alpine flowers, wetlands and outstanding views of Fiordland's biggest mountains are the rewards for an hour or so of steady but well-graded climbing.

- Take a day trip (or longer) to Doubtful Sound/Patea. You'll cross beautiful Lake Manapōuri, drive over a mountain pass, then board another boat to explore remote Doubtful Sound/Patea – three grand scenic treats in one. Wildlife watching (dolphins, seals, penguins) is a likely bonus.

- If taking a day trip to Milford Sound/Piopiotahi, start and finish your journey in Te Ānau. Some tours travel to and from Queenstown, a long and arduous journey.

- In summer drive the Milford Road out of peak hours to avoid congestion on the road and at roadside attractions. An early or late morning start is recommended.

- If your time and fitness is limited, the view across Lake Manapōuri from Shallow Bay offers a glimpse of Fiordland's majesty. Getting there is an easy 1.5 hour walk through beech forest on a section of the Kepler Track.

- During or after heavy rain, wherever you are in Fiordland, check out the waterfalls.

the drone of small planes on the Queenstown/Milford flight path is incessant, to the point of distressing some climbers and trampers seeking a wilderness experience in the valleys below.

Scenic flights aside, several companies offer charter services for tramping, hunting, fishing and photography. Many also help with search and rescue, avalanche control and conservation work.

Fishing

Fiordland's lakes and rivers are stocked with brown and rainbow trout. Several local fishing guides offer a range of options – day trips or multi-day expeditions, fly fishing, trolling and spinning, many of them promoting catch and release. A fishing licence is required for fishing in the park.

Hunting

There is a long traditional of recreational hunting in Fiordland. Introduced red deer, wapiti (elk) and chamois are present. Red deer built up to such numbers in the mid 20th century that their browsing of native vegetation became a threat to the natural environment and government hunters were employed to reduce numbers. During the 1970s and 1980s aerial hunting by helicopter was a major business.

Permits are required for hunting and hut tickets must be obtained if staying in a park hut. These are available from Department of Conservation offices. There is a limited season for hunting wapiti. Hunting guides are available, as are boat and plane charters to hunting spots.

Mountain biking

Bikes are not permitted in the park except on legal roads. However, there is an excellent mountain-biking opportunity on the Borland Road, towards the southern end of Fiordland. This road was constructed in the 1960s to service a transmission line from the West Arm Power Station, on Lake Manapōuri. It is unsealed, steep in places and subject to slips, high winds and, in winter, snow and ice. Nonetheless it is very scenic. From the park entrance the road climbs some 20 km to Borland Saddle, a stunning viewpoint, then descends a further 25 km into the Grebe Valley. For adventurous cyclists (very adventurous!) a track has been blazed from the road-end to Percy Saddle. From here a road descends to West Arm of Lake Manapōuri. It is necessary to carry bikes for at least an hour over this difficult section. Boat transport is available from West Arm to Manapōuri township.

Milford Road

The 119 km road from Te Ānau to Milford Sound/Piopiotahi is regarded as New Zealand's most outstanding alpine drive. The mountain-lined road leads alongside Lake Te Ānau, traverses the grass- and forest-covered flats of Eglinton Valley then climbs to the Divide. From here the landscape becomes even more majestic, dominated by the sheer granite walls of the Darran Mountains. After the Homer Tunnel (1.2 km long, 945 m above sea level) the road descends steeply through dense coastal rainforest to the journey's grand finale, Milford Sound/Piopiotahi.

Driving time is 2 to 3 hours each way, but allow a full day at least to explore the viewpoints, short walks and dramatic landscapes. The road is likely to be very busy with cars, coaches, campervans and minibuses. Congestion is rife during the peak season (October to April), both on the road and at Milford Sound/Piopiotahi. There is serious avalanche danger during winter and spring near the Homer Tunnel, so complying with the 'no stopping' restrictions is a very good idea. The road is sometimes closed from Marian Corner (near the Hollyford Valley turn-off) because of adverse conditions, particularly in winter.

There is limited accommodation at Milford itself for backpackers and campers, and several roadside campsites in the Eglinton Valley. Te Ānau is the closest township and last fuel stop.

Several local operators provide tours that connect with most cruise options on Milford Sound/Piopiotahi.

Southern Scenic Route

Follows the eastern park boundary from Te Ānau to the south coast and Invercargill. There are many short walks and interesting scenic and historic points along the 200 km route, and side trips through the park to the forest-surrounded Lakes Monowai and Hauroko.

Information

Getting there: By road, SH6 from Queenstown or Invercargill, then SH94 to Te Ānau (2 hours from both Queenstown and Invercargill). Alternatively via the Southern Scenic Route from Invercargill (2.5 hours). Several companies provide regular coach services from most main centres, including Queenstown, Invercargill and Dunedin. By air, Queenstown and Invercargill are the closest major airports; some companies provide small-plane services to Te Ānau.

When to go: Summer for tramping and alpine flowers, winter for climbing, any time for other activities, though snow and avalanche danger may restrict travel on the Milford Road during winter and spring.

Climate: Mild summers with long twilight hours. Cold winters, but generally more stable weather. The sea has some warming influence on the coast. Expect snow in winter and heavy rain throughout the year.

Accommodation and facilities: Te Ānau township has a full range of accommodation (from luxury lodge to backpacker and camping), restaurants, supermarkets, banks, shops, petrol and other services. Accommodation is also available at Manapōuri, Te Ānau Downs and Milford.

There are 60 park huts, ranging from small bivouacs with no facilities to large, well-equipped huts. Great Walks huts have hut wardens, gas cookers and lighting and a daily radio schedule with park staff. There are several self-registration campsites throughout the park.

Commercial ventures: Guided walks, scenic cruises, wilderness cruises, scenic flights, water and air transport services, guided kayaking trips, guided fishing, guided hunting, diving trips, equipment hire (tramping and kayaking).

Further reading: Fiordland Parkmap; Milford Track Parkmap; Kepler Track Parkmap; NZMS 260 series topographical maps A44, A45, B41 to 47, C40 to 46, D39 to 44, E43; park brochures; *The Darrans Guide: An Alpine and rockclimbing guide to the Darran Mountains*, Murray Judge and Hugh Widdowson (New Zealand Alpine Club); *Moir's Guide South*, edited by Robin McNeill.

Special conditions: In winter and spring, be wary of avalanche danger on the Milford Road in the vicinity of the Homer Tunnel, and on the Milford Track. Park staff can advise on safety precautions. Year-round you'll need to take insect repellent to deter sandflies.

Visitor centres: Fiordland National Park Visitor Centre, on the Te Ānau lakefront, provides weather and track information, hut tickets, Great Walks bookings, hunting permits, maps, brochures and a small retail shop specialising in books on natural history and recreation in the park. There are also displays, an audiovisual show and community museum. The i-SITE centre in Te Ānau offers information and bookings for activities and accommodation in the region.

Fiordland National Park
Visitor Centre
Cnr Lakefront Drive and
Manapōuri Highway
PO Box 29
Te Ānau
Phone 0-3-249 7924
Email fiordlandvc@doc.govt.nz
Open daily 8.30 am to 6 pm or
8 pm (summer) or 4.30 pm
(winter)

Fiordland i-SITE Visitor Centre
Lakefront Drive
PO Box 1
Te Ānau
Phone 0-3-249 8900
Email fiordland-
iSITE@realjourneys.co.nz
Open daily 8 am to 7 pm
(summer); 8.30 am to 5 pm
(winter)

Rakiura National Park

Location: Stewart Island/Rakiura, south of the South Island

Features: primeval island wilderness ■ dense rainforests ■ isolated inlets ■ beaches and dunes ■ wetlands ■ granite mountain domes ■ exceptional wildlife ■ offshore island sanctuaries

Activities: short walks ■ tramping ■ sea kayaking ■ nature tours and cruises ■ birdwatching ■ hunting ■ fishing ■ engaging socially with an island community

Stewart Island/Rakiura is one of the world's largest unspoilt forested islands, and 85 per cent of it is protected in Rakiura National Park. The island is New Zealand's third largest – nearly 170,000 ha in size – and yet barely 400 people live there, mainly in and around Halfmoon Bay.

The park is a wilderness of dense podocarp rainforests, freshwater wetlands, sand dunes, granite mountains and tundra-like alpine vegetation. Some 170 smaller islands and rocky islets are scattered along the coastline. Some of these are refuges for New Zealand's rarest birds, such as the heavyweight of the parrot world, the kākāpō.

Rakiura provides a rare chance to experience primeval New Zealand. Day walks explore the forests and coastline near Halfmoon Bay and on the open sanctuary of Ulva Island. The Rakiura Track is a Great Walk, while an 8 to 10 day northern circuit is one of the longest remote experience walks in the country. Sea kayaking and cruises are other options; nature tourism forms a major part of the livelihood of the residents. Fishing and aquaculture are also important.

About the park

Rakiura, the park's name and the island's Māori name, means 'land of the glowing skies'. It refers to the magnificent sunsets, as well as displays of the southern lights, Aurora Australis, often seen from the island's shores. The name Rakiura is also an abbreviation of Te Rakiura a Te Rakitamau – 'the deep blushing of Te Rakitamau', recalling Te Rakitamau's embarrassment on hearing that the woman he sought to marry was already engaged, then his deepening blush when he asked after the woman's sister and heard she too was engaged.

Another traditional name for the island is Te Puka a te Waka a Māui, 'the anchor of Māui's canoe'. This refers to the story of the fisherman Māui and his use of the South Island (Te Waka a Māui, 'the canoe of Māui') as the canoe from which he caught the North Island (Te Ika a Māui, 'the fish of Māui').

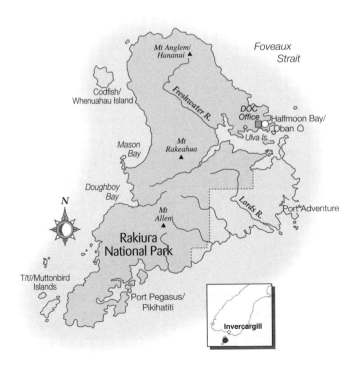

People in the park

Māori people have lived on the island since the early 13th century. Rakiura is in fact recognised as being the southernmost island to have permanent settlement in all of Polynesia. The island's waterways and surrounding sea provided an abundance of food, such as eels, inaka (whitebait), shellfish, fish, sea birds and fur seals. Young sooty shearwaters (tītī, muttonbirds) were particularly valued and today local Māori maintain traditional harvesting rights of tītī on the tribally owned Titi/Muttonbird Islands.

The island retains many sites of very strong cultural and spiritual significance. In accordance with the settlement between the Crown and Ngāi Tahu in 1998, original Māori names have been restored to a number of key places, and special associations with Mt Anglem/ Hananui have been recognised by the placing of a tōpuni, an overlay of tribal values, on the mountain.

European settlement on the island has been spasmodic since the 19th century, starting with short-lived sealing and whaling camps and an unsuccessful attempt to develop a ship-building industry. The milling of native timber lasted for 70 years, until 1931, but large-scale operations were fortunately thwarted by the island's distance from mainland markets.

Mining and farming were even less successful ventures thus fishing, nature tourism and, more recently, marine farming have proven to be the main economic ventures for the small island community.

Glorious isolation

Set apart geographically on the subantarctic edge of New Zealand, Stewart Island/Rakiura has largely been left to nature's devices. It harbours a treasure chest of unmodified ecosystems and habitats, a haven for rare plants and endangered wildlife.

The dense rainforests that cover much of the island are the southern-most podocarp forests in the world. Nine podocarp species grow here, mixed with kāmahi and southern rātā, though several forest species that are common elsewhere, for example beech, kōwhai and māhoe, are absent here. More than 80 species of fern grow on the island, with tree ferns in particular thriving in the wetter gullies. A hardy band of wind- and salt-resistant tree daisies cling to the exposed coastal fringes.

The most abundant bird species are tūī, bellbirds, fantails, grey warblers, South Island tits and brown creepers. Interestingly, these birds are most prolific not in the remote forests of the park but around Oban, because of the township's varied food sources and proximity to Ulva Island open sanctuary. Less common park species are red- and yellow-crowned parakeets (kākāriki), South Island kākā, Stewart Island weka, Stewart Island robins, South Island saddlebacks (on Ulva Island) and, one of the island's most special residents, southern tokoeka.

Southern tokoeka are also found in Fiordland, but unlike their cousins the island's kiwi feed during daylight hours, making Rakiura one of the few places where it is possible to see kiwi in the wild. One of the reasons they have survived has been the absence from the island of the ferrets and stoats that have affected mainland bird populations.

On the exposed west coast, windswept beaches are backed by sand dunes of staggering proportions. Behind the 15 km expanse of sandy beach at Masons Bay are dunes 3 km wide that climb to an impressive height of 150 m. These vast dunes support a range of threatened native plants, including the sand tussock *Austrofestuca littoralis*, a rare creeping herb *Gunnera hamiltonii*, the shore spurge *Euphorbia glauca* and the gold-coloured pīngao. Further north, beaches with the telling names of Smoky, Ruggedy and Hellfire face the prevailing westerlies, which have over hundreds of years blown sand up to 20 km inland.

In contrast, the lee, eastern side of the island is punctuated with several sheltered inlets, drowned river valleys now surrounded with mature native forests that grow right to the water's edge. The largest is Paterson Inlet/Whaka a Te Wera, which cuts a swathe deep into the centre of the island and rates as one of the largest and least modified estuaries in the country. Many marine species, including kina (sea eggs), sea cucumbers, starfish and brachiopods live in the inlet, which is also a habitat and nursery for at least 56 species of marine fish.

The inlet of Freshwater Valley follows a fault-bounded trough west into the island's rugged interior. Freshwater habitats are among the island's most complete natural ecosystems and the native fauna they support is outstanding. Unlike most New Zealand waterways, the island's rivers are free of introduced trout, which eat native fish. The 15 species of freshwater fish living here include large numbers of giant kōkopu (this largest of all galaxiids is now rare in mainland waterways).

The highest place in the park is Mt Anglem/Hananui (980 m), an imposing 9 km massif of igneous diorite rock that dominates the northern interior. Many of the herbs, dwarf shrubs and speargrasses present here grow nowhere else; 21 of the island's 23 endemic plants grow in the alpine zone. Flowering herbs, bog lily, *Celmisia* daisies and mountain buttercups also flourish on Mt Anglem/Hananui.

The weathered granite domes of the Tin Range, dominating the southern skyline, are more akin to landscapes in Rio de Janeiro or Yosemite Valley. Intriguingly, the alpine shrublands high on the Tin Range are home to a colony of coastal wading birds – one of New Zealand's most endangered species, the southern New Zealand dotterel. Unlike its northern cousins, which breed and feed on coastal sands, this subspecies travels from mountaintop to coast to feed. By 2004, after a decade of intensive control of feral cats during which conservation staff battled through snowstorms and gales, the population of southern New Zealand dotterels had risen from 64 birds to just over 200.

The Tin Range was also the last mainland home of the world's only flightless parrot, the kākāpō. During the mid 1980s, conservation staff caught the last 40 of these highly endangered birds and, to save them from feral cats, relocated them to offshore island refuges.

Island wildlife habitats

Codfish Island (Whenuahou) is a 1400 ha nature reserve lying off the remote north-western coast of Stewart Island/Rakiura. Kākāpō, fernbirds and short-tailed bats live in this refuge, which was in 1998 cleared of rats using leading-edge island management techniques.

While Codfish Island (Whenuahou) is closed to the public, the more readily accessible Ulva Island is managed carefully as one of New Zealand's few open sanctuaries. Located in the national park in Paterson Inlet/Whaka a Te Wera, the 250 ha Ulva is covered with magnificent podocarp forest that has been cleared of rats and had a number of rare and endangered species released. Visitors who follow strict quarantine measures can land on the predator-free island and observe several species of native birds now uncommon in mainland forests, such as saddlebacks and yellowheads.

What to do

Short walks

There is an excellent variety of walks around Halfmoon Bay. While just outside the national park boundary, these walks offer glimpses of history and wildlife. Other walks are on Ulva Island open sanctuary; regular boat services run from Golden Bay. Brochures give full details.

Fuchsia Walk/Raroa Reserve (Halfmoon Bay) 1 hour return

A gentle wander through fuchsia forest then unmodified podocarp forest, with native bird life prolific.

Harrold Bay and Ackers Point Lighthouse (Halfmoon Bay)

3 hours return

Follows a coastal road and then a walking track to Ackers Point, a great viewpoint of Paterson Inlet/Whaka a Te Wera and offshore islands. If here at dusk, watch the sea birds coming home – little blue penguins and, in late summer, tītī (sooty shearwaters) – after a day of fishing. At Harrold Bay the walk passes one of New Zealand's oldest buildings, Ackers Cottage, built in 1835 when the bay was a busy ship-building base.

Top tips

- Take a trip to Ulva Island. Listen to birdsong as it sounded on the mainland before humans and animal predators.
- Kayak silently through the sheltered waters of Paterson Inlet, one of New Zealand's biggest and most pristine harbours.
- Look for sea birds on a scenic cruise along the coastline of the park, an area that supports breeding populations of at least 20 different sea birds, including petrels, shags, penguins and tītī (sooty shearwaters).
- Take a snorkel or scuba dive in the clear, pristine waters of Te Wharawhara/Ulva Island Marine Reserve.
- Engage with the friendly island community; join them in a round of golf on the world's southernmost golf course.

Whalers Base (Paterson Inlet/Whaka a Te Wera) 20 minutes return

A former Norwegian whalers' base in Prices Inlet, within Paterson Inlet/ Whaka a Te Wera, where Antarctic whale chasers were repaired in the 1920s and 1930s. Many relics remain. Getting to the inlet involves a 20-minute boat trip from Golden Bay.

Boulder Beach and West End Beach (Ulva Island) 3 hours loop

Watch and listen for kākā, kākāriki, saddlebacks, yellowheads, Stewart Island robins and South Island riflemen, along with common native birds. The forest is dominated by rimu, kāmahi and the brilliant red-flowering southern rātā.

Flagstaff Walk (Ulva Island) 20 minutes return

There's also lots of human history on Ulva, from early days of milling, boat building and when the island served as post office for the irregular mail boat from Bluff. Flagstaff Walk leads to a fine outlook of Stewart Island/Rakiura, at the point where a flagstaff was erected so residents of Paterson Inlet could be signalled when the mail boat arrived.

Longer walk

Garden Mound–Little River–Lee Bay (Halfmoon Bay)
4 to 5 hours return
A mix of great views, the Little River outlet, coast and the striking Link Sculpture that marks the entrance to the park. The time given above is from the park visitor centre, and includes some road walking.

Multi-day tramping trips

Rakiura Track 3 days
A circuit from Halfmoon Bay, following the coast, climbing over a ridge then traversing the shore of Paterson Inlet/Whaka a Te Wera. The track can be walked in either direction. There are two huts (Port William and North Arm) and three campsites. Features are coastal outlooks, beach walking, tidal flats, and rimu and kāmahi forest. The track visits sites of former Māori kāika (hunting camps). The start is accessible by foot from Halfmoon Bay, or sea kayaks and water taxis can be hired for access to huts and campsites.

North West Circuit 8 to 12 days
This is a remote, challenging 125 km walk around the northern coastline of Stewart Island/Rakiura. There are 10 huts, spaced between 6 km and 15 km apart. The tracks are notoriously muddy, but on the bright side they pass through varying landscapes: dense rainforest, impressive sand hills, regenerating mānuka forest and subalpine shrublands. A side trip climbs to the subalpine meadows of Mt Anglem/ Hananui, the high point of the park (6 hours return from Christmas Village).

Southern Circuit 4 days
This can be added to the North West Circuit or accessed by boat transport across Paterson Inlet/Whaka a Te Wera. There are five huts spaced 10

km to 18 km apart. It is a remote, challenging circuit requiring a high degree of fitness, tramping experience and self-reliance. Parts of the circuit are easily flooded. Landscape features include wetland/swampy areas, shrublands and boglands, beach and sand dunes.

Sea kayaking

Paterson Inlet/Whaka a Te Wera is a special spot for kayaking, with some 10,000 ha of sheltered, forest-fringed inlet, two navigable rivers and 20 islands to explore. There are four Department of Conservation huts accessible from the inlet. The more sheltered waters at Port Pegasus/ Pikihatiti and coastal explorations of Stewart Island/Rakiura are further kayaking options. Guided kayak tours are available and kayaks can be hired. Winter weather is generally more settled for kayaking.

Paterson Inlet/Te Whaka a te Wera and Ulva Island

New Zealand conservation scientists have developed a worldwide reputation in offshore island restoration and species recovery work. Many islands have remained free of introduced animal pests, whose forest browsing and egg and chick predation have significantly damaged mainland habitats. On other islands, scientists have perfected techniques to eradicate pest animals such as rats, possums and mice, thus enabling forest recovery and the reintroduction of rare and endangered species to these safe, predator-free sanctuaries.

To avoid the risk of reinvasion of animal pests, many of these island sanctuaries are closed to the public. Ulva Island, the largest of many islands within Paterson Inlet/Te Whaka a te Wera, is one notable exception. After rats were eradicated in 1996 the Department of Conservation designated the 266 ha island as an open sanctuary, which means the island's plant and bird life can be experienced in independent or guided day visits by the public, provided precautions against rat reinvasion are taken.

Visitors to Ulva are greeted with the sights and sounds of a thriving bird population. In addition to all of the birds found in the forests of the main island, a number of less common and endangered birds have been reintroduced. These include South Island saddlebacks, yellowheads, Stewart Island robins and South Island riflemen. These birds can be seen and heard on several short walks leaving from the island's wharf, as well as along the 3 hour loop track to Boulder Beach and West End Beach.

Ulva Island is in the heart of Paterson Inlet/Te Whaka a te Wera, one of the largest and least modified estuaries in the country and home to at least 56 species of fish. In 2004 a significant area of the inlet, centred on Ulva Island, was declared as Te Wharawhara/Ulva Island Marine Reserve. No marine life within the 1075 ha reserve can be removed or harmed. In addition, 9000 ha of the remainder of the inlet has become a mātaitai reserve, managed by tangata tiaka (caretakers) from the Stewart Island/Rakiura community. Mātaitai reserves can be managed through by-laws that allow (or prohibit) the taking of fish, seaweed or other aquatic life.

This level of protection, of both Ulva Island and the waters nearby, should ensure this very special natural environment and the life it sustains will remain safeguarded for all time.

Special precautions are necessary to protect Ulva Island. Rodents can arrive on offshore islands in personal luggage and badly packed food. To reduce risks, seal food containers and boxes with tape and tie bags tightly. Check your packs or bags immediately before leaving for the island. When both loading and unloading, check packages and bags for rodent sign, such as droppings and gnaw marks. If you are unsure, unpack, inspect and repack. Licensed nature guides and water taxi operators are required to follow strict precautionary guidelines and to ensure all passengers do the same.

Diving

A warm current flowing to Stewart Island/Rakiura from the Great Barrier Reef attracts a greater diversity of marine life than would usually be found at this latitude. An underwater forest of bladder kelp (unique to these waters) extends some 70 m from deep rocky reefs to the surface and is home to many species of fish. Snorkelling and scuba diving are both rewarding, either from charter boats or off the coast, and there are good diving spots in Ulva Island Marine Reserve. Charter boats will organise the trip to suit, whether visiting deep areas for scuba dives or anchoring off remote beaches or reefs for snorkelling.

Fishing

Fishing, in particular for blue cod, has long provided a livelihood for the people of Stewart Island/Rakiura. Today several operators, some of them retired commercial fishermen, run full-day or half-day fishing trips for visitors. Shellfish, such as scallops and paua (abalone), can be gathered around the coastline – within legal limits, of course.

Fishing and shellfish gathering (or damaging of any marine life) is not permitted in the Ulva Island/Te Wharawhara Marine Reserve. In addition, the remainder of Paterson Inlet/Whaka a Te Wera is part of a mātaitai reserve, which prohibits commercial fishing and manages recreational fishing to ensure the sustainability of this traditional Māori food-gathering area. As a result, most charter fishing operators limit trips to the open coast.

Hunting

The presence of the only readily accessible whitetail herd in the southern hemisphere makes the island is a popular hunting destination. Some red deer are also found in the north-west of the island. The Department of Conservation administers 35 hunting blocks and an open hunting zone within the park. The blocks are limited to one party (maximum of 10 hunters and total party size of 12) for a maximum of 10 days. Applications for blocks are accepted up to a year in advance. Contact Department of Conservation, PO Box 3, Stewart Island.

Hunters can stay in park huts (with prepurchased hut tickets) or specifically established hunters' camps. Outside the park there are 13 blocks in the Rakiura Māori Land area. Permits for these must be obtained from the Rakiura Māori Land Trust, PO Box 77, Bluff.

Information

Getting there: Daily flights from Invercargill (20 minutes) and daily ferry services from Bluff (1 hour). Several charter operators run boat services from Bluff, and some fixed-wing and helicopter operators are licensed to land on beaches below the high-tide mark, and at the Long Harry, East Ruggedy and Hellfire Pass hut sites.

When to go: Any time. In summer there are very long daylight hours, but the reverse applies in winter. Winter is more settled for kayaking.

Climate: Weather is changeable throughout the year, with few extremes except for persistent westerly winds that often rise to gale force. Generally warm summers, cool winters but with few frosts or snowfalls. Average temperatures are 16°C in summer and 9.9°C in winter. Cloudy and wet – rain falls most days but the annual average (1600 mm) is not high.

Accommodation and facilities: Halfmoon Bay accommodation includes upmarket lodges, hotels, motels, home-hosted, self-catering and budget backpackers. Also in Halfmoon Bay there are a few cafés and craft shops, an activities centre with outdoor equipment for hire, and one general store. There is no bank or ATM on the island.

Commercial ventures: Guided walks and overnight tramping trips, nature cruises and tours, glass-bottom boat tours, birdwatching tours with New Zealand Birding network operators (Ulva Island, pelagic birds, kiwi spotting), sea kayaking tours, diving charters, fishing charters, scenic flights and aerial tramping/hunting access, vehicle hire.

Further reading: Stewart Island Parkmap; NZMS 260 series topographical maps D48, E48, F48, C49, D49, E49, C50, D50; park brochures; *Stewart Island: A Rakiura ramble*, Neville Peat; *Stewart Island Explored*, John Hall-Jones; *Stewart Island New Zealand*, Les Pullen; *Stewart Island Plants*, Hugh D. Wilson; *Rakiura*, Basil Howard; *An Island Called Home*, Sheila Natusch.

Special conditions: When visiting Ulva Island ensure boats and bags are checked to prevent accidental reintroduction of mice, rats, cats and other pests, including plant and seed pests.

Track surfaces are varied, with long sections of deep mud. Some areas are also prone to flooding. Tramping boots are essential and gaiters are strongly recommended. Sandfly repellent is also recommended.

Hunting bookings should be made early, especially for the March to June period. Bookings are accepted up to a year in advance.

Cellphone coverage throughout the island is unreliable.

Visitor centre: The park visitor centre at Halfmoon Bay provides weather and track information; hut tickets, maps, brochures, trip intentions forms; and advice on hunting, the marine reserve and mātaitai regulations, transport and guided trips to Ulva Island and tramping/hunting destinations and air access to parts of the island. Maps, emergency locator beacons and storage lockers can be hired. There are also interpretive displays on the island's biodiversity, cultural history and recreational opportunities.

Rakiura National Park Visitor Centre
Main Road
Halfmoon Bay
PO Box 3
Stewart Island
Phone 0-3-219 0002
Email stewartisland@doc.govt.nz
Open daily 8.30 am to 7 pm (26 December to 31 March);
shorter hours during the rest of the year